52 Lessons from Network Marketing

By Jerry West

No part of this publication may be reproduced, distributed, transmitted in any form or by any means, including photocopying, recording, or other electronic or mechanical methods, without prior written permission of the author, except in the case of brief quotations embodied in critical reviews and certain other noncommercial uses permitted by copyright law.

This book is sold with the understanding that its contents are provided for informational purposes only. In practical advice books such as this, like anything else in life, there are no guarantees of income or success made. The author of this book is not engaged in rendering legal, financial, business, or any other form of professional advice. If any form of professional advice or expert assistance is required, the services of a competent professional person should be sought. The author specifically disclaims any liability that is incurred from the use or application of the contents of this book.

This book is dedicated to my wife, Amy. I am forever grateful for your unconditional love, support and encouragement. I love you.

For Network Marketing tips and advice, I invite you to follow and connect with me on Facebook by visiting:

Facebook.com/JerryWest.biz
Facebook.com/52LessonsBook

You are invited to join the official...
"52 Lessons from Network Marketing" Facebook group.

Enter to WIN a FREE personal coaching call with Jerry West! Here's how to enter:
Post a selfie holding a copy of this book and use
#52LessonsBook

To purchase more copies of this book for you and your whole team please visit: **www.52LessonsBook.com**

Edited by: Michelle Dieber
Cover design: Jim Bitten, 44 Communication Design

Table of Contents

Introduction

Introduction

I am finally doing it. I am sitting here writing the book I have been thinking about; seemingly forever. You see, as of the time I am writing this, I have been a network marketer for just over six years and just recently became a full-time network marketer and multiple six figure earner in the industry. I am heading towards seven figures, and who knows, perhaps I will be one by the time you read this book.

I have learned so many life lessons through Network Marketing and I want to share them with everyone. These lessons will help you in the industry and many can be applied to nearly any situation in life. I was not always a positive person, nor was I born a leader. I became who I am today by experiencing all the ups and downs of Network Marketing and persisting until I was successful.

I have been through struggles in my life; mostly stemming from lack of self-confidence and belief in myself. I started school at a young age and was immature in comparison to the other kids. Later in elementary school I was bullied and began to develop an inferiority complex. This led to alcoholism and drug abuse in my early adulthood, and the drinking continued into my married life.

I went to college to be in radio and quickly realized I was never going to make enough money to provide a nice lifestyle for my family. I moved on to a marketing position for a local phone book publisher and ended up sitting in a grey cubical for nearly 9 years. Most days, I just stared at the clock waiting for the work day to end so I could go home and have a drink.

I'll be the first to admit I was not the best husband and father during these years. Thankfully, in September of 2010 that job did me a favor and fired me. I felt such relief when this happened as I now had new life. Little did I know at the time that this would be a huge turning point for me.

I went on to start a sales job at a local community newspaper where I started selling advertising to small business owners. I began attending networking groups to meet more prospects and started to notice that the people I was meeting were all motivated to improve their lives. They were all out looking for more connections, more referrals and more business.

One day, at a small, local networking group in my village, a man showed up and was very excited about the company he was with. He began talking about residual income and people earning monthly checks with numbers that seemed outrageous to me. I couldn't imagine how anyone would be able to earn more money in a month than I was making in a year. I had to find out what the heck he was talking about.

I set up an appointment to meet with him and the rest is history. Thanks to this man introducing me to Network Marketing, my entire life has been transformed over the past six plus years. During that time, many lessons were learned through trial and error, struggle, sacrifice and perseverance. I failed in several companies, owned a direct mail franchise that went under and put me into major debt. I was forced to file bankruptcy and faced the uncertainty of not knowing when my next bill would be paid.

Through all of this, I never gave up on myself. No matter what, I always got back up, brushed myself off, and applied the knowledge I had learned. Every mistake I've made has made me stronger and more successful. It's all part of what has made me who I am today. My goal with this book is to share some of these lessons I have learned with you, in hopes that they will resonate and move you closer to reaching your personal goals.

I wanted to write something that anyone could read, enjoy and learn from, but also be able to use to discuss a different lesson every week of the year. This is what I came up with and I hope that it adds a ton of value to your journey.

Lesson 1: Express Gratitude

There are many reasons people start this journey and they all have one thing in common. They all want more out of life and are looking for a way to achieve it. They have resolved themselves to the fact that whatever they are currently doing is most likely never going to do it for them. They are tired of living paycheck to paycheck, being in the rat race, wasting endless time commuting to a job they don't care about, and working tirelessly to help somebody else get rich. This is where the old adage "sick and tired of being sick and tired" comes from. They are convinced that there *has* to be a better way.

Even though I agree there is a better way, I would also like to point something out. There's a lot more to life than meets the eye. Every day we wake up, open our eyes, and take a deep breath is a gift. There are so many things we should be grateful for that we take for granted on a daily basis. It could be our health, loved ones, family, house, automobiles, food on the table, running water, breathable air, and even our job. Instead of appreciating what we have, we often fall into the trap of thinking what we have isn't good enough and being envious of others. This is a long, miserable road to travel.

Today is a gift and tomorrow isn't guaranteed, so we need to be thankful for these things and express gratitude every single day. Take time every day to appreciate everything you have while you work towards achieving everything you want. Every morning when you wake up and every evening before you go to bed, express gratitude for all that you have. Remember, there are people out there praying to be in the position that you are in.

Appreciate every single little thing; express gratitude daily, and you will be a much happier and more positive person. People that lack the ability to appreciate the small things are hardly ever successful and never feel fulfilled in life. This is a simple exercise that you absolutely need to practice on a daily basis. You cannot expect more blessings to come into your life until you've learned to appreciate the ones you've already received. Do not let a single day go by, without expressing gratitude towards these blessings. Only then, can you invite more in.

Action Steps and Discussion:
- Write down every little thing you can think of that you may currently be taking for granted.
- Read this list daily and express gratitude for having these blessings in your life.

Lesson 2: Attitude is Everything

What type of attitude do you have when you wake up in the morning? Do you hit the snooze button a few times or are you excited to jump out of bed and take action? Are you happy with the work you are doing at your job or do you dread having to go there? Your attitude at the beginning of the day has a huge effect on your results in life and your Network Marketing business.

The great thing is that we get to *choose* our attitude. Every day when you wake up, you have a choice. You can lay there in bed dreading having to get up, or you can jump up and be excited for another day. Instead of having negative feelings about going to work and all the things you have to do, you can choose to look at the positives. What can you do today to move your life in a more positive direction? What negatives can you choose to ignore so that you may focus on more positive activities?

Whining and complaining isn't going to change a darn thing. Having a bad attitude towards your day will only magnify the things you dislike and your negative feelings will continue to grow stronger. Choosing to have a positive attitude towards everything may not change your life overnight, but it certainly will feel different right away. If you have a positive attitude every day, over an extended period of time, it will transform your entire life.

Action Steps and Discussion:
- Identify anything in your life that you are currently unhappy with or have a negative feeling about. Focus on how you can take positive actions daily, in

order to change these things or at least change how you think about them.

- Identify anyone you spend time with that may be poisoning your mind with negativity like complaining, justifying and making excuses. Detach yourself from these people. Identify people who are positive influences in your life and make an effort to associate only with them.

Lesson 3: Raise Your Belief

Your belief level is one of the biggest determining factors in the success of your business. How strongly do you believe in Network Marketing, the company and products you are associated with, and most importantly, yourself? Your ability to grow your Network Marketing business stems all from how strongly you believe in all of these things.

Belief in the Network Marketing industry and business model is a must. If you are new to the industry and not really sure what you are doing, or maybe you've tried a few companies and haven't had much success yet, you must continue to believe in what you are doing. Building belief every day will show others confidence. Have you ever seen someone pitch a Network Marketing company and seem unsure or desperate? This comes from lack of belief. If this is you, plugging into your team calls, events and trainings will help raise that belief. Work closely with others who are having success and duplicate what they are doing. Remain consistent no matter what your results are. These activities will all raise belief.

Do you 100% believe that the company and products you are representing are life changing? This is so important when it comes to growing a business. I have seen people involved in companies where they do not actually use the products or necessarily even believe in them. If you are finding that the products or service are not even benefitting you, how do you expect to enthusiastically and genuinely promote them to someone else? People can smell a fake from a mile away. The most important sale you will ever make in

Network Marketing is the one you make to yourself. You have to be completely sold on the fact that the company you are with and its products or services will vastly improve people's quality of life; physically, financially, or both. Developing your own success story and being a product of the product will raise your belief through the roof.

Finally, we get to the most important question: Do you believe in yourself? It may be difficult to do if you haven't had much success yet. The bottom line is, no matter what level you are at, you absolutely must believe in yourself. Setting time aside each day for personal development, affirmations, meditation, and exercise will help tremendously with this. When you consistently feed positive information into your brain and your body feels fit and energized, your belief level in yourself will be at its peak. Work on improving yourself daily!

Action Steps and Discussion:

- Schedule time every day for personal development, at least 15 minutes up to an hour.
- Do something every day to make your body feel energized. Go for a walk or run, hit the gym, or even do pushups and sit ups at your home. Even 15-20 minutes of physical activity per day will make a difference. Force yourself to do this even if you don't feel like it.

Lesson 4: Positivity vs. Negativity

We've already discussed the importance of waking up with a positive attitude. Let's discuss the difference between focusing on positives vs. negatives and the impact this can have on your business. Our lives are exposed to thousands of influences on a daily basis; some positive, some negative; and we choose which ones to focus on. The same is true within our Network Marketing businesses.

There are many things that can go wrong within your business. I think we can all agree that massive growth and momentum are great problems to have. These can also lead to shipping and delivery issues, customer service issues, and conflicts between different personalities on your team; to name a few.

These things will inevitably pop up and it's your choice how to respond to them.

Being negative about problems will not only stunt the growth of your business, it can absolutely destroy your business if you allow it. Take a look at your own behavior and answer these questions: When there's a shipping issue, do you complain and poison the group with negativity? If a product shows up at your home damaged, do you blast it out on social media? Are you airing your dirty laundry on social media and using it as a venting platform? Do you allow yourself to be drawn into drama and arguments in chat groups, posts, fan pages, and social media groups? If you are doing any of these things it will prevent you from experiencing positive growth and it will sabotage any success you are having, if any. You cannot spread negativity into the universe and expect positivity to come back to you.

On the other hand, if you maintain a positive attitude no matter what the situation, you will experience much more growth as a person and in your business. When there's a problem, find a solution. When something unfavorable happens in your business, remain positive and do not let it sway you. When people in your team are complaining be a shining light of positivity, and show them what true leadership means. Being positive regardless of circumstances is one of the most powerful qualities you can possess. You may have heard the saying, "positive energy goes where positive energy flows". It's the truth. The more positivity to put out into the universe, the more that will come back to you. Be a magnet for it!

Action Steps and Discussion:

- Review your social media posts and determine if you are producing positivity, negativity, or both. Next, clean up anything that is negative. Going forward, do not post anything unless it has a positive purpose.

- After every interaction you have with another human being, take a few minutes to reflect on how it went. It could be a conversation at the grocery store, a phone call, or an interaction at work. Determine whether you were being positive or negative. If the other person was being negative, did you feed into it? Or were you able to remain positive and deflect the negativity? Learn from these interactions and make a mental note of what you need to improve the next time.

Lesson 5: Celebrate Every Success

One of the biggest mistakes people make, whether they are new to the industry or not, is not recognizing their own progress. I once had an affiliate on my team tell me she was disappointed because she was only making a dozen or more new customer sales and sponsoring a handful of new business partners per month. My response was to tell her she was doing fantastic and should be proud of all the success she was having.

Every success you or your team has in this industry should be recognized and celebrated. It's a very big deal when somebody makes their first sale, sponsors their first distributor, reaches a monthly goal, hits a new rank, or does something outside their comfort zone; whether it results in a sale or not. Any time someone in my team experiences personal growth, I am right there to pat them on the back. If they are doing their first-ever live video on social media, you can bet I am on it encouraging them, cheering them on, and telling them how proud I am once they are done.

It's easy to get caught up in wanting to reach high ranks and not recognizing the little things we accomplish on a daily basis that help us get there. This business is about consistency and perseverance. There isn't a success story out there that happened overnight; even though it may sometimes appear that way. If you dig deeper into anyone's story, you will eventually uncover the struggles they went through to get there. There was a time when they were celebrating their first sale, their first live video, and their first tiny victory. Make a huge deal out of every small victory because they all deserve to be celebrated!

Action Steps and Discussion:

- Write down every accomplishment in your business and personal life no matter how small and give yourself accolades for achieving them.

- During the week make a concerted effort to recognize any time you or somebody on your team does something positive. Go out of your way to make a big deal out of every one of them.

Lesson 6: Drop Your Excuses

Excuses can stop even the smartest and most educated people from reaching greatness. Most of these excuses are made up in our own minds and we don't even realize how lame they are. They can be popular opinions or misconceptions that our friends, family, and society has led us to believe. If you are going to be successful in Network Marketing, you need to drop them all.

How many times have you heard yourself or someone else say I don't have time for that, I'm too busy, I don't know the right people, I live in a small town, nobody I know is interested, nobody I know has money, it's too expensive, I can't afford it, I'm not a sales person, I'm too shy, I don't want to bug anyone, those things never work, I heard it's a scam, and so on. The list of excuses is never ending. This may hurt for some of you but I'm going to say it anyway. These are all extremely lame!

These are all things you need to get past if you are ever going to succeed in *anything*, really. We all have the same 24 hours, so how is it that *you* don't have time? Lame! It's all about how you prioritize your time. What is more important to you: a television show or creating a legacy for your family? You may say that nobody you know is interested or has the money. Lame! Go out and find people that are ready to get started today. You are not a sales person, yet you recommend movies, restaurants, recipes, and many other things to your friends? C'mon now, that is a lame excuse! These things don't work or they are a scam? Seriously? That's why so many people are doing it successfully without being arrested. Lame!

Do you see where I am going with this? The sooner you decide to drop all of your excuses and just go for it, the faster you grow personally and professionally. Not a single top income earner out there whined and complained their way to the top making lame excuses along the way. Make the choice to drop all of the excuses immediately and watch how much happier and more successful you will be!

Action Steps and Discussion:

- For the next week, pay close attention to everything you say and do. Take notes every time you catch yourself making an excuse for something.

- Go through your list at the end of the week, identify each excuse that you made and think about how you could have handled each situation differently. Apply what you have learned next time.

Lesson 7: Remember Your Why

One of the first things we are told when we join a Network Marketing business is to write down your why. This is extremely important because it's your why that keeps you going no matter what happens. If the only reason you are doing something is for the money then you will have a hard time staying inspired and you won't have much, if any, story to share with people.

Stories are what sell in Network Marketing. The most powerful stories are the ones that include some kind of struggles that were overcome. If you are able to take a negative situation and succeed in spite of that, then you will have a very powerful story. It can be financial hardship like bankruptcies, repossessions and foreclosures. It can be family and health related struggles that you were able to push past and succeed anyway. *This* is what inspires others to become part of your team.

Whenever you are dealing with self-doubt or lack of motivation it's always important to go back and remember why you started in the first place. Remind yourself of all the reasons you wanted to do this and what it will be like when you succeed. They say your why should be so strong that it makes you cry. Nothing can stop a person who is on that powerful of a mission.

Action Steps and Discussion:
- Write down the reasons why you originally started this business, and any other reasons that have become a part of your story along the way. Read these reasons every morning and evening to remind yourself of your why.

Lesson 8: Take Action

The fundamental key to success in any Network Marketing business is taking action. When I say taking action, I am referring to income generating activities. Many people will watch training videos, get on webinars, study the comp plan, learn all the details about the products, and ask tons of questions. These things are all well and good, but none of them are moving you towards your goals.

When it comes to taking action in Network Marketing, the "actions" being referred to are prospecting and presenting. Exposures to your products and opportunity are the gateway to success. The more people you expose, the more customers and affiliates you will sponsor, and the better you will get at talking to people. The only way to get better at prospecting and recruiting is to do it more often.

There's a saying that goes like this: "It is better to be ignorance on fire than knowledge on ice". This refers to someone who joins, immediately takes action, and learns the rest as they go. When you focus on taking action everything else falls into place. If you aren't good at talking to people, take action and you'll get better. If you don't understand the compensation plan, take action and you'll start to *see* how it works. If you don't know every little detail about your products, take action and you'll learn them when people are asking you questions. Are you getting the point?

You don't have to know everything there is to know when you start your business. All you need to do is take action with income generating activities and you'll learn the rest soon enough; trust me.

Action Steps and Discussion:

- Keep a log of your daily activities for a week and identify how much time you are spending on busy work, or non-income generating activities. Be completely honest with yourself.

- Readjust your agenda to include income generating activities 80% or more of the time.

Lesson 9:
The First Person You Lead is Yourself

This was a tough lesson for me to learn and I imagine it's the same way for many. We all come into this business in different ways and most of us are influenced in one way or another, by our sponsor. Some of us are lucky enough to join great leaders right out of the gate; others join those that are just getting started and not sure exactly what to do. A few of us come in under someone who may be negative and not a good role model, or worse, someone who quits the company and leaves us looking for guidance.

The real truth in Network Marketing is that you do not need an upline to become successful. Of course, it's extremely helpful and rewarding to be working alongside people that are passionate about the products and opportunity; just like you are. You should consider yourself blessed if you are in a situation with great leadership and role models above you. Even if you aren't, that doesn't mean you will not be successful. No matter what your situation is, you will need to become the upline yourself; at some point. Success in Network Marketing is all about leadership and the first person you lead is yourself.

When I finally became serious about Network Marketing, I joined a company that I was with for over two years and finally started to achieve decent levels of success. Through the help and influence of my upline, I began to attract higher caliber marketers into my organization. We hit some major momentum about eight months into the business and things took off. Our team exploded for about nine months and then we hit a wall. Team volume began to shrink and nothing we did was turning it around.

A few months into the downfall my sponsor decided to leave the business and join a competitor; which, at the time, I viewed as a "shiny ball" on social media. I was devastated and felt like everything was lost. Then I remembered a quote that my CEO at the time, would always use: "The first person you lead is yourself."

I decided right then and there that I no longer needed an upline. From that day forward I proceeded as if I was the top ranked leader in the company regardless of my actual rank or title. I began working extremely hard on improving my leadership skills and setting an example for others. I no longer would accept excuses or negativity and I fully accepted accountability for my own business. That day, *I* became the upline.

Even though I have since left that company and went on to achieve massive success in another company, the one I am involved in now, that is still growing incredibly, that lesson has always stuck with me. I will continue to teach it to others so that they may break free of the stigma that they need to depend on anyone else to help build their business. All you need to do is become the upline *yourself* and help others build their businesses and achieve their goals. Once you decide to do this, you have no limits.

Action Steps and Discussion:

- Identify anything you currently depend on your upline for, on a regular basis and begin to take responsibility for as many of them as you can. Only go to your upline when you *really* need help.

- Begin volunteering to talk on team calls, train and present at meetings, and speak on stage at events. If you want to be a leader, you must start doing the things leaders do.

Lesson 10: Remain Humble

What do you think most people are looking for in a sponsor? If you said somebody they think can help them get what they want, you are onto something. I would also add to that, somebody who is relatable, somebody who has a great story, somebody who cares about others, somebody who remembers where they came from, and somebody who is humble and kind.

Success and money can have a negative effect on some people. It's important to make sure that this never happens to you. We have all seen the arrogant type of network marketer on social media flashing cash, trash talking about jobs, and basically insulting and putting down anyone that hasn't reached their level of income or decided to do what they are doing.

How does this make you feel when you see this? I can tell you it didn't make me feel good or attracted to that person in any way.

This type of flaunting behavior makes people feel as if they are below you and that is the last feeling you ever want to give anyone. Someone like this is not relatable to anyone and whether they know it or not, they are repelling a lot of great people from joining their team. The way that we rise to the top is not by belittling those that don't have what we do; instead, it's by lifting others and taking them on the journey with us.

If Network Marketing takes you from bankruptcy to multi seven-figure earner, it is extremely important to always remember where you came from. Never forget the unpaid bills, collection calls, repossessions, foreclosures, and feelings of self-doubt that you may have had when you started. There are tons of people out there, right now, feeling the same way and waiting for someone humble to show them a way to change their situation. Be that kind and humble person; extend your hand, and show them there's a better way.

Action Steps and Discussion:

- Make a video telling your story without leaving out any details. Make it as real as possible. Post it on your social media outlets and share it with others. You will be surprised how many people relate to the same struggles you have gone through in your life. This is powerful!

- Perform at least three random acts of kindness for people that you don't know yet. Then, introduce yourself and make new friends!

Lesson 11: Authenticity

When someone is new to the industry, they do not yet have a story to tell people. I have seen people make up all sorts of things in this situation. They may tell untruths, or embellish how much money they've made so far, and even hype things up, creating unrealistic expectations for their prospects. Unfortunately, social media often becomes a vehicle for painting an inaccurate picture.

I'm sure you have heard the phrase "Fake it until you make it" on more than one occasion. This refers to someone that hasn't "made it" in the industry, yet their posts on social media indicate otherwise. Perhaps they are showing fancy cars and houses that aren't theirs, or making false income claims.

All of these things are designed to fool others into joining them because they are after the lifestyle that is being portrayed.

The truth is this really isn't an effective strategy to build a Network Marketing business. Even if people join you they will find out the truth soon enough. If you really haven't "made it" yet, it will become quite apparent very quickly that you are not able to help them, and that you are lying. You are also missing out on a lot of great people by faking it because most intelligent people can see right through the facade. It's also not very relatable or inspiring to many, due to the lack of back-story that got you to where you "are" today. There's nothing to relate to because it's all been made up.

Authenticity, on the other hand, will take you anywhere you want to go in this business.

People love a powerful, inspiring and *real* story. If you are genuine and real, it isn't going to matter to the right people, if you haven't had much success yet. Tell people your story about how you got started, why you chose to do this, and where you plan to go with it. Give them something to relate to, that allows them to see how they may be able to change their own lives.

If you have had success, tell them about the struggles, the hard times, what it was that finally made you take a chance and put yourself out there. Share the stories of others in your organization and how they inspired you. Authenticity is a key that will unlock many doors for you; always remember to use it.

Action Steps and Discussion:

- Do a live video on social media where you tell your story to your followers.

- Review all content you are putting out there and ensure that it's real, authentic and relatable.

Lesson 12: Duplication

Duplication is one of the most important things in Network Marketing. We need to teach new distributors a simple system that they can duplicate and teach others to do the same. In a perfect world, we would all sponsor two, who sponsor two, who sponsor two, and so on. But guess what? It's not a perfect world and it never works that way. Duplication isn't easy.

Many people that join will try to reinvent the wheel instead of following a system. They feel more comfortable sticking with what they know, rather than doing what they are being taught; which is often uncomfortable. People will create their own websites and company social media pages, they will design their own brochures and presentations because they don't like the company provided materials.

They will start using their own system because the one in place makes them feel uncomfortable and they don't want to perform and follow the necessary steps. They will even skip steps; not get on calls, not attend events, blow off training, and then blame the company or their upline when they don't succeed.

You can't control what everyone else does, but you can control what you do. This is why you should always do things that are duplicable for the average person. Use the company websites and videos, get on all the calls, attend all the events, present the products and opportunity the way the company teaches. Your team will do what they see you do. If it's duplicable, they will have a much better chance at succeeding and teaching others to do the same. Always follow the system and use the tools that are already in place.

Action Steps and Discussion:

- Make sure you are plugged into every company call, event and training.

- Resist the urge to create anything on your own and only use the company provided websites, marketing materials, and presentations.

Lesson 13: Motivation & Inspiration

To be successful in Network Marketing, you need to be motivated and inspired. Motivation can come from all different sources; such as famous motivational speakers, your upline, company leadership, and even doubters and haters can motivate you. The most important motivation comes from within.

The ability to self-motivate is extremely important because without motivation to take action, you will continue to procrastinate and never really get started. It takes self-motivation to get started and you must continue to take action; no matter what the results are. Nothing ever happens as fast as we would like it to. This is why it's so important to maintain the same motivation and enthusiasm you had when you started. If you treat every day like it's your first day in the business, always being super excited and focusing on your why, then you can't help but to succeed.

Motivation often comes from inspiration. People often tell me that my story inspires them and they look forward to reading my posts every day. This was one of the main factors that inspired and motivated me to write this book. I knew that if I produced a book filled with inspiring messages for every week of the year, it would allow me to help so many more people. Helping others is something that inspires me more than anything else in the world.

Inspiration can also come from within. Perhaps you have recently been through a struggle in your life or simply have a strong desire to achieve more. Maybe you have recently evaluated your own life up until this point and felt that you could be doing so much better. These things can inspire you to make a change and start making different choices. Self-inspiration can motivate you to make radical changes in your life. If other people start thinking you are crazy and obsessed with success, then you know that you're on the right track.

Action Steps and Discussion:

- Do something every day that inspires you to take action. This could be reading a book like this one, watching a motivational video or listening to motivational audios. The more positivity you feed your brain, the more inspired and motivated you will be.

- Eliminate anything that is taking away motivation and positive thinking. Replace any negative going into your brain with positive.

Lesson 14: Overcome Fear

Are you familiar with that feeling when there's something you know you need to do, yet for some reason you just can't bring yourself to do it? It could be calling a very influential prospect, following up with people you have already spoken with, or messaging a friend that you know can benefit from your products. There's a reason you are holding back. It's called fear; better known as False Evidence Appearing Real.

Being afraid to fail or get a negative response stops so many people. They just don't want to deal with it so they avoid taking any chances. The problem with this is that fear grows stronger, the longer you allow it to stick around. Every time you hold back, you are feeding the muscle of fear instead of the muscle of action. We all feel fear; even the most successful people in the world. The difference is that they act in spite of the fear.

Fear creeping in is a clear indication that you need to take immediate and decisive action. The only thing that squashes fear is action. When you take action immediately, you build the muscle of action and fear doesn't have a chance to grow. Every time you do this, fear gets smaller and you grow stronger. Train yourself to pounce on fear every time it rears its ugly head. Take action immediately!

Action Steps and Discussion:

- Every time you feel fear, force yourself to take action immediately. Do not give fear any opportunity to grow and get stronger. Do not think about it; just go ahead and do it!

Lesson 15:
Happy Customers Make the Best Affiliates

One thing that turns a lot of people off from Network Marketing is feeling like they are being pitched a business opportunity. The fact is, not everyone wants a home business. I could argue that everyone needs to have one, but that's a conversation for another time. For today, we will simply say that not everyone wants one; which is the truth.

Often times, when you approach somebody in an attempt to sign them up for a business, you will miss out on the chance to help them as a customer. They may feel that purchasing from you will result in constant bombardment to sell the products as well. Nobody wants to be pressured into something. Even if you do manage to pressure somebody into joining your business, they are most likely going to disappoint you and do nothing. The only way to get someone to do something is to make them *want* to do it. If they don't want to do it, they won't; whether they join you or not.

On the other hand, if you present a product to someone that solves a solution for them, then they will be more than willing to try it. Most people feel good about helping others and if the product appeals to them, they will want to help you. Once they become your customer, you should treat them like gold. Customers are the lifeblood of your business and should be treated as such. If you continue to treat them well and they continue to get great results using the products, and they see the success you are having, eventually they will ask you how they can make money too.

When a customer asks you how to upgrade, it's the best kind of affiliate or distributor you can get. Here is someone that is already sold on the benefits of the product and it was their idea; not yours, to start their own business. Now, they will feel comfortable going out and telling the world about what your company has to offer and how it can be life changing. This is what happens when you approach things from a product standpoint and care more about helping the other person; rather than helping yourself.

Action Steps and Discussion:

- Make a list of people that you know can benefit from your products or services. Set a time to talk or meet for a coffee with each person and introduce only your product or service to them. Do not mention a business opportunity!

Lesson 16: Don't Believe the Hype

Hype is something that a lot of new network marketers fall for when results aren't coming fast enough for them. They start to look at other opportunities, thinking that they will be easier to achieve success and overlook what they really need to be improving on; which is themselves. Instead of doing the work and pushing themselves outside of their comfort zone, they chase "shiny balls" and believe in false promises. They justify these things in their own minds and to others.

Hype can come in many forms. They may see another network marketer promoting how easy it is to make money in their company, as opposed to others. How many times have you seen somebody say that their company is designed for the average person to make money? To that I say: aren't they all? You can start as an average person in any company and earn extra income, a full time income, or even become a six or seven figure earner; if you do the work and improve yourself daily.

Hype can show up as promises of spillover, timing and positioning. While these may very well be things that can benefit you, they are not going to build a business for you. There is no magic "done for you" business out there that will build itself without you doing the work. I see people fall for it all the time. Heck, I fell for it back when I was a newbie. Unfortunately it's simply not true; otherwise everyone would do it and we would all be millionaires, doing zero work.

If it doesn't make sense and it looks too good to be true then it usually is exactly what it appears to be. If anyone ever tells you that you can make a lot of money by doing very little or no work, they are lying. No matter which company you are in, where you are positioned, what the timing is or how much spillover you receive, you are not going to escape doing the work. Trust me, this comes from experience. Believe in genuine excitement, but do not ever believe in hype.

Action Steps and Discussion:

- Look through social media and find five examples of pure hype and five examples of legitimate excitement and success. Learn to recognize the differences.

Lesson 17: Changing Lives

We hear it all the time in Network Marketing. Every affiliate and company claims they are changing people's lives. It can be physically, financially, spiritually, or any combination of the above. After all, isn't that what it's all about? Everyone that starts has a "why" and our goal should be to help them achieve it. Many people start this business with the goal of earning extra income and there's always a much stronger "why" behind it. If there isn't a strong "why" then how can we change their life?

There's a saying that goes like this: "People don't care how much you know; until they know how much you care". With that being said, how much do you genuinely care about others? It's really hard to build a successful

Network Marketing business if you aren't willing to get up close and personal with people. You need to know and understand why they got involved and what needs to be done in order to help them reach their initial goal. Once the initial goal is reached, their "why" can change. Every level that is reached can change the "why" and increase the goal. You must care enough to stay in tune with these changes and continuously help your team take the next step. Every achievement, no matter how small, can be life changing.

If you are truly focused on changing people's lives by helping them achieve one "why" after another, then you are on the road to massive success. You will have to be the person who encourages and inspires them to continue no matter what the obstacles. People hit plateaus in all kinds of journeys such as weight loss, working out at the gym, dealing with various health issues, or simply growing their Network Marketing business. In order to change their life, you have to be the one who helps them believe in themselves enough to keep going; no matter what stands in their way. You must be a source of positivity that they can turn to when things are not going as planned.

To change lives, you have to be a servant leader who is always focused on improving and finding solutions. Always be aware of your team's ever-changing reasons for being involved and continuously adapt to help them move forward.

Action Steps and Discussion:

- Go through every personally sponsored distributor and every leader you work closely with on your team. Do you know what everyone's current "why" is? Make sure you contact each individual and find out what their current goals are.

- Team exercise: Have everyone in your team write down their current goals, what their current "why" is, and dates by which they want to achieve them. If you want to be really creative, have each person on your team create a vision board.

Lesson 18: Focus vs. Scatterbrain

We've all seen that distributor who's involved in multiple Network Marketing companies at the same time. It's like the guy with the trench coat who has something for everyone, watches on one side, pocket knives on the other, and various other items for sale in the pockets. He may make a buck or two here and there but chances are, he's never going to make it big because he lacks focus.

When you chase multiple rabbits at the same time, chances are, you will never catch any of them. You will also look like a scatterbrain to anyone who is looking to start their own home business. People are out there; looking for someone who can help them reach their goals and realize their dreams. Who do you think is a more attractive sponsor to them-

Jerry West

someone who is focused on building one business or someone who is trying to build four at the same time?

Splitting your focus in many different directions is more of a roadblock than it is a pathway. It's extremely difficult to gain momentum in any one direction if you are always switching gears and making turns. Much of Network Marketing success is based on personal development and leadership. How many strong and successful leaders do you see promoting multiple opportunities at the same time? It's a very short list, if it is even a list at all.

Putting the blinders on and remaining focused is one of the key factors that helped me to achieve my first major breakthrough. When you are laser focused, others start to see you as a leader who can help them reach the next level. Focus is one of the most important things you can teach your team to duplicate. When your team is completely focused, it's so much easier to build massive momentum.

Action Steps and Discussion:

- Evaluate everything you and your team are doing and determine if you are focused.

- If you are not focused, make some tough decisions. Eliminate things you are not passionate about and choose one direction to pursue. Then put on the blinders!

Lesson 19: Run with the Runners

People ask me all the time about the best way to motivate their team members. The absolute best way is to lead by example. I'm sure you have heard the question- if your team did what you did today how happy would you be? The answer had better be extremely happy and excited! Your actions are the biggest motivator for your team; as they will do what they see you doing.

What can we do with people who aren't moving at all? I have done it all and seen it all in this situation. There have been times when I would be messaging and calling people daily, in an attempt to motivate them. I could not understand why they were not working on their business. After all, this is the vehicle they have chosen to accomplish all of their goals and dreams. Aren't their dreams important enough to them, that they would want to take action on them? The answer is that it's ultimately up to them. You can't let people that are standing still prevent you from moving forward.

I have also fallen into the trap of "messiah mode" where I start building their business for them; thinking that they will be motivated when they see the results. I've actually helped people to advance their rank or status within the compensation plan, watched them celebrate at the end of the month, and then do absolutely nothing the next month. If moving up in rank didn't motivate them, nothing will. The truth is motivation has to come from within them. There's nothing you can do to force someone into taking action unless they want to. This is why it's so important to keep moving forward and focus on building your business; no matter what.

I once attended a company event where they discussed this topic on stage and illustrated it with the example of a three-legged race. They brought two pairs of people up to the stage. The first pair were both standing up and ready to run, while the second pair had one person standing and the other laying on the ground attached at the leg. When the speaker signaled for them to go, the first pair ran quickly across the stage while the second pair struggled with one person trying to drag the other along. Obviously the pair that won the race was the first pair, as both of them were running together. The second pair didn't get very far at all.

This is an extremely important lesson to understand. You will not reach your goals by attempting to drag unwilling participants along with you. It's not your responsibility to save people who do not want to save themselves; or, to do the work for those who are no willing to take action. Always focus all of your time and energy on building with those who are running *with* you. If you do this, your business will gain momentum so much faster and some of those that were left behind may eventually wake up and start chasing you.

Action Steps and Discussion:

• Go through your entire team and make a list of the people who you should be spending the most time building with. Focus at least 80% of your time on these people.

• Evaluate your daily habits and decide if you are doing what you would want your team to be doing every single day. Write down what you would like your team's daily habits to be and start by completing this list yourself, daily.

Lesson 20: Desire

Starting a Network Marketing business and having the desire to actually do what it takes to build one are two different things. Many people that join Network Marketing for the first time do not realize what they are getting themselves into. There's a lot of hard work, sacrifice, learning new skills, dealing with failure, changing of mindset, and overcoming obstacles involved, and that's just to name some of the trials and pitfalls people will run into.

You really have to ask yourself if your desire is strong enough to push through everything that you will have to go through. Are you prepared to deal with negative people and naysayers? What if those naysayers are the people closest to you? Is your desire strong enough to keep going when things are not moving anywhere close to as fast as you thought they would? Are you willing to continue investing more than you are making and sacrifice things like watching television and sleep until you have a breakthrough?

The people that achieve huge success in this industry are the ones who have the strongest desire. They are the ones who keep going and remain positive; no matter what comes their way. They know what their goals are and will not stop at anything until they are achieved. They work on their mindset daily and are constantly learning and improving their skills. They have the wherewithal to overcome setbacks and unexpected circumstances. They are able to rise above drama and negativity at all costs. If this describes you, then there's a great chance you have the desire to make it to the top.

Action Steps and Discussion:

- Evaluate your daily habits and determine what your true priorities are.

- Start making necessary changes to your habits and hold yourself accountable.

- Write down why you originally started this business. Be sure to include what your goals are and when you want to accomplish them by. Post this in a visible place where you will look at it daily.

Lesson 21: Analysis Paralysis

It's amazing how many people get stuck in this phase that prevents them from moving forward. They feel that they must know every detail before lifting a finger. They will research every ingredient in the product, what it does, how it works, spend hours watching training videos and webinars, and ask endless questions about the compensation plan. They can get stuck in this rut for days, weeks, months, or even years. It's called analysis paralysis and it's a black hole you want to avoid at all costs.

Let's be real here. You may have heard the phrase "it's better to be ignorance on fire than knowledge on ice." I understand the need or desire to learn about everything and know what you are talking about. It's a natural human emotion. It's also true that all the knowledge in the world will not earn you a single red cent unless you take action. People who take action right away, whether they know everything or not, are the ones who get paid and rank up very quickly. The ones who get stuck in endless training mode may be learning, but they are certainly not earning.

The truth is you do not need to know everything, or really much of anything, to take action and start sharing your product and opportunity with others. Most companies have systems and tools in place to grab attention and pique interest, inviting, presenting and closing for you. Why try to explain everything yourself when there is a video that does that for you? Why struggle answering questions when you can get your upline leader on the phone with your prospect?

It's called learning while you are earning. The more you watch that video, the better you will understand how things work. The more you listen to how your upline talks to people and answers questions, the more you will improve and begin to do it yourself, and helping others do it. I encourage you to always take immediate action; whether you feel ready or not. You can train and overanalyze all you want, but the only way we truly learn is by doing and repetition. Take action now!

Action Steps and Discussion:

- Review your daily routine and determine if you are spending too much time on trainings, webinars, and overanalyzing things. If you are, start changing your daily habits to income generating activities.

- Make a list of daily actions that will bring in income. Hold yourself accountable by checking off each item on the list, every day, when it has been completed.

Lesson 22: Never Dare to Compare

Here's the scenario: A big leader joins your company and hits multiple ranks in their first month. There are all kinds of accolades and recognition going on all over social media. Sure enough, people in your team start coming to you complaining about the rapid success and demand to know what it is they are doing wrong. They want to know why they have been in the business much longer and haven't even hit the first rank, while this person is now standing on stage holding up a big check. Jealousy is at an all-time high.

All they can see is what is going on in the immediate present. What they are failing to see, are the struggles this person has gone through to reach this accomplishment. This leader is not an overnight or even a one-month success story. This is someone who has spent years learning the right skills, perfecting their craft, building their network, getting knocked down only to stand up again and get back to work. They have sacrificed watching TV, going out with friends, and a lot of family time and sleep to get where they are. They have been consistent daily, weekly, monthly and yearly for an extended period of time.

I admit it, there have been times that "comparitis" has gotten the best of me. I can tell you from experience that it doesn't serve you well nor does it help move your business forward. All it will do is stop you in your tracks and stall any momentum you have. The main reason being that you are in the first few chapters of your journey. This big leader has gone through all of that and now is in a very late chapter. In other words, it's not an apples to apples comparison. It's more like apples to grapefruit.

The best cure for comparitis is heavy doses of personal development and mindset training for you and your team. Focus on where you are, what your goals are, what your why is, and what you need to do in order to move your business. Focus on overcoming the obstacles that are standing in your way; which many times, are our own limiting thoughts. Personal development is huge in bringing us out of this funk. Work on yourself every single day and do not spend another minute comparing yourself to someone else. We are all on our own journey; focus on yours.

Action Steps and Discussion:

- If you are currently feeling jealous or comparing yourself to someone else, simply let it go. Pace yourself on a strict personal development regimen and focus on the actions you need to take in order to advance your business.

- Discuss comparitis and the pitfalls with your team. Recommend personal development to them and set up an accountability group for anyone who needs it. Show them that you are focused on building your team and helping them build theirs.

- Celebrate the success of other teams in an extremely positive way and show your team that you want *everyone* to win. This helps maintain an abundance mindset for everyone.

Lesson 23: Waiting for the Right Time

I think you may already know what I'm going to say here. The best time to start was yesterday and the second best time is right now; so let's do this. The only day we have to do anything meaningful with is today. Yet people are always putting things off until tomorrow or a future date. They have convinced themselves that there's a better time than now to get started. Here's a news flash for you: there isn't.

Prospects will do this all the time as a stall tactic. They need to wait until they get paid, until after the holidays, when things slow down a bit, when there's suddenly more time to finally focus on doing something new. They fool themselves into believing that they have less time than others when in fact they have the same twenty four hours per day that everyone else has. It's usually these same people that have time to watch television, time to shop, time to complain, and time to do whatever will waste more time. These are not the people that you want in your business. I wouldn't write them off completely, but I would keep moving ahead and let them come back to you when they "have time" to do so. People change; I did, but you cannot stand still and wait for them.

Then there's your business partners who did actually join and are now waiting for the right time to take action. It's the same story, waiting for after vacation, until school is over, when things lighten up a bit. Well, we both know things will never lighten up. We are all busy. This is more about priorities and fear than anything else. When this happens, remind them why they started in the first place. Ask them if the actions they are taking now, or not taking, are helping them move closer to their goals.

Is fear stopping them? If so, I suggest daily personal development. I had to work on my mindset every single day for years to get to where I am now. I still work on my mindset daily whether it's listening to an audio book in my car, reading a book, watching a motivational video, composing my own posts to help others, or even writing this very book. Every positive word and thought that enters your mind helps to get you moving. Positivity in, equals positivity out and encourages action and the best time to take action is right now.

Action Steps and Discussion:

- Take a look at your daily habits and what you are telling yourself. Are you holding yourself back?

- Are you telling yourself lies in order to avoid the things you know you need to do?

Lesson 24: Goal Setting

Goal setting is one of the major keys to success; yet most people never get around to doing it. When I say "goal setting" I mean definitive goals with dates attached to them. A lot of people will say they want to make ten grand a month, pay off debt, make extra income, create a college fund, buy a new car, buy a new home, or retire themselves and their spouse, but they never take those wishes seriously enough to write them down with a deadline next to them. Yes, you read that right, a deadline by when they wish to accomplish each goal.

The hard truth is that a goal that is not written down with a date and a plan on how to get there is merely a wish. If you are not going to commit to it, you may as well wish it happens and do nothing else. Since you are reading this book I know you are not like that. You are serious about making your goals a reality. What better way to prove how serious you are by writing them down and giving yourself an ultimatum. Write them down and read them every day so that your mind knows what you plan to do, how you plan to do it, and by when you want to do it.

Another great way to visualize your goals becoming reality is to create a vision board. You can print images from the internet, cut them from a magazine, or take pictures of things and print them. Pin all of these images on a board that is in a very visible location. You want to make sure that you are seeing and visualizing these goals on a daily basis. I have even seen people use vision board apps on their phones. Imagine visualizing your goals becoming reality every time you look at your phone, which I'm imagining you do a lot since you are a network marketer.

It's one thing to have goals, and another to actually be visualizing them as being reality along with an action plan. Make this part of your daily routine and they will drive your passion.

Action Steps and Discussion:

- You should know exactly what you need to do after reading this; but in case you don't, write down all of your goals and leave them in a place where you can see them.
- Read all of your goals every morning when you wake up and every night before you sleep.
- Create a vision board with images of your goals placed in a very visible place in your home.

Lesson 25: Fear of Failure

The thing that stops most people from taking action is fear of failure. As human beings, the last thing we want to do is fail at something; so we make the unconscious choice not to try. The worst is when we convince ourselves that we are trying our best and doing everything we can when we actually aren't. I have had people on my team tell me they are trying hard every day when all they are doing is wishing. I know, because - you guessed it; I have been guilty of this myself in my early days of Network Marketing.

Every day you are building a muscle. It's either the muscle of action or the muscle of inaction. Whichever one you feed is the one that gets stronger. The longer you allow fear to stop you from taking action, the stronger the fear will get until it has you frozen. No amount of wishing, waiting or hoping is going to unfreeze you. In order to break free from this, you absolutely must step outside of your comfort zone and take action right away.

How many times have you had a conversation with someone and they bring up a problem that your product, service or opportunity can solve? When you get that feeling in the pit of your stomach that you should say something, when you feel that fear start to creep in, that's a clear indication that you need to take action as quickly as possible. Taking action will immediately squash the fear and you'll have an overwhelming feeling of relief; regardless of the outcome. Taking immediate and decisive action is the only thing that squashes fear. The more you take action right away, the bigger that muscle will get and fear will shrink.

Successful people still feel fear; they simply know it's an indication to act and they always take action in spite of it. Train yourself to know that feeling and to react with action every single time. Your muscle of action is the most important one you can work on in Network Marketing. Action trumps everything. It's the gateway to massive success and you must walk through it day in and day out. Make your action muscle so strong that fear of failure is no longer a thought in your mind.

Action Steps and Discussion:
- Pay extra close attention to what you are feeling throughout each day and when you start to notice that fear of failure creep in, immediately squash it with action.

- Make note of every time you don't take action although you wish that you did or feel you should have. Use this as motivation to squash the fear next time you are in those same situations.

Lesson 26:
Prison of What Other People Think

The saddest place a person can live is inside the prison of what other people think. This can stop us from following our hearts and being true to ourselves. When we take actions and make decisions mainly to protect ourselves against the judgement of others, it leads to a very unfulfilling life. Living just to please others and not bother anyone with our goals and dreams is a self-confidence issue. The cure for this is a heavy dose of personal development.

When you start to work on your mindset daily, your belief in yourself will increase. Typically, the people you are trying to appease are not really your circle. There's a whole circle of people out there that are just like you; they enjoy the same things, have a similar vision, and share common interests and goals. You'll never attract these people unless you start being true to yourself and to do this, your mindset must be strong enough to let some people go.

The people you hang around with the most are the ones who will determine who you are and how far you can go. With that being said, take a look around you and see who you are spending the most time with. Does this group of people support your goals and dreams? Are they living the lifestyle that you want? Are they positive, encouraging and motivating? If you are answering "no" to these questions, then you need to change your circle of influence.

In order to be successful in Network Marketing, you have to break free from what society accepts as the norm and start marching to the beat of your own drum. Show others that you are unbreakable and have strong convictions about what you are doing. Do not allow people that think small to take your power away and steal your dreams. Think and dream bigger than them and you will attract a whole new crowd of people that are on the same wavelength with you. Your vibe will always attract your tribe. Make sure your vibe is strong enough to free yourself from the criticism of naysayers and start attracting the praise and attention of those who align with your vision.

Action Steps and Discussion:

- Make a list of the 5-10 people that you spend the most time with. Determine if they support you, align with your vision, and are living a lifestyle that you want. Write next to each name a "yes" or a "no" in order to decide who you need to spend more time with and who you need to see less and/or let go.

- Make another list of 5-10 people that you currently do not spend time with who you would like to get to know. Reach out to each person and start a conversation. See if you can meet up for coffee or schedule time to chat on the phone. These are the relationships you should focus on building.

Lesson 27:
Personal Development & Growth

One of the best things about Network Marketing is that it gives the average person an opportunity to achieve above-average and sometimes even massive success. In short, a Network Marketing business gives you the chance to earn more income than any job could ever pay you. I love the income, time freedom and options that it has allowed me to provide for my family. That being said, I think most professional network marketers would agree with me, that the personal development and growth aspect alone makes it well worthwhile.

Personal development has been a huge part of my journey. Without it, I could not have made it through all of the failures, unexpected twists and turns and setbacks. There will be many highs and lows in building a Network Marketing business and you must be mentally strong enough to remain positive in order to persevere. To be clear, you will not have much of a chance to become successful in this industry unless you are working on yourself and improving your mindset daily.

There are many ways to work on your mindset. You can read books, listen to audio books, watch motivational videos, listen to podcasts, and attend seminars and events to name a few. Take advantage of and utilize anything that strengthens your mindset, reinforces positivity, sparks income generating activities and helps you to rise above the noise. What you feed your mind on a daily basis is what it will produce. Positivity in, equals positivity out. This is the cornerstone to all of your future success.

No matter how you choose to feed your mindset, consistency is the key. You must find methods and manage your time so that it becomes part of your daily routine. I have found audio books to be my favorite because when I am home, it's tough to set time aside to sit there and read, mostly because I am always in action mode. I have found that using the time I am in my car to listen to audio books is the way to go. Instead of listening to the radio filling your head with music, mindless chatter, or even worse, the news, you can turn your car into an automobile university. Whatever you decide to do, just make sure it's done consistently every single day; whether you feel like it or not. It's well worth investing the time and resources to make it happen.

Action Steps and Discussion:
- Look over your daily routine and schedule in time where you will be doing

personal development each day. I highly recommend replacing TV time with either personal development or doing income generating activities.

- Decide today, to turn your car into an automobile university and listen to a book every time you are in your car. Resist the urge to listen to music and the news.

Lesson 28: Support Your Friends

Do you support your Network Marketing friends that are in other companies? I have seen many people that support their friends whenever they can and quite a few others that see people in other companies as competition. Choosing to support others will always get you farther than doing the opposite.

I always support my friends no matter which business they are in and I become their customer whenever I have a need for something they are selling. I would much rather purchase a product or service from a friend of mine, than head out to a big box store. They are working hard to accomplish their goals just like I am, and that is something worth supporting. I have many friends in other companies that are my customers because I never make them feel like they need to quit their business and join mine. I make people feel comfortable being my customer and in the meantime, I am cheering them on in their business.

When you support people and help them regardless of what team or company they are in, it shows that you have an abundance mindset. This is a key trait that great leaders in the industry have. Supporting your friends will build strong relationships which can lead to amazing things in the future. You never know when someone will be looking for a change of scenery. When they are, do you think they would prefer to partner with someone who always supported them? Or do you think they would prefer someone who saw them as competition and never spoke to them until they were looking? I know my answer.

Everyone knows somebody that needs what you have to offer. Even if people you support never decide to join your team or buy something from you, chances are, they will refer others to you. The way to receive referrals is by giving and always being supportive.

Action Steps and Discussion:

- Take a look at all of your friends in other companies and see what they are offering. If there's something you need or can use- support them by becoming their customer.

- Review your actions and decide if you are operating from an abundance mindset. Make any necessary changes to your actions and habits.

Lesson 29: Presenting & Training

The best leaders in the industry are great at presenting. They were not always great at it; they *became* great by repetition. They stepped outside of their comfort zone and presented whether they felt comfortable doing it or not. They did it so many times that it became natural to them. I'm not saying they don't get nervous or butterflies in their stomach anymore. Most successful people still feel fear when it comes time to take action. The difference is that they have trained themselves to act in spite of fear by doing it so many times that the fear has been squashed.

Part of being an outstanding presenter is having a powerful story to tell and delivering it effectively. When you join this industry, you begin to develop a story. There's the story about how the products or services have helped you, and then there's the story about how the opportunity has changed your life. Most great stories include times of struggle, setbacks and disappointments that the person was able to overcome. Many people are struggling and can relate to going through tough times. It's extremely inspiring to listen to a story about struggle and overcoming it from someone they can relate to. This will make them want to hear what you have to say.

Learning how to train others to duplicate what you are doing is also an important skill. To do this you must also be relatable and have a great story. When people trust you and are inspired by you, they will listen to what you tell them to do. Training effectively takes many hours of repetition as well. The more you focus taking action to build others up, the better you will get at it. There's no bigger reward in this industry, than watching someone who you trained and mentored, achieve success. It's the best feeling in the world when someone advances in rank status or hits a big bonus and you played a large part in helping them get there.

When you learn to present and train well enough so that your entire team is winning, that's when *you* will be winning big-time. You will notice others start to follow in your footsteps and become great leaders as well. This is what makes Network Marketing a truly amazing industry.

Action Steps and Discussion:

- If you are not currently doing any presenting or training, speak with your upline and tell them that you intend to up your leadership game. See if there are any calls you can speak on or other opportunities.

- Take out a note pad and write down all of the highlights of your product story and opportunity story. What have you accomplished? What have you overcome to get there?

Lesson 30: Embrace the Struggle

There are no overnight success stories; even though it sometimes may appear that way. We see somebody come into the business and crush it right away, pass us in rank, and then we wonder how they did it so fast. The answer is: they didn't. What we are failing to recognize, are the years of hard work and consistence that led to this person being able to launch so fast. We are only seeing the end result instead of looking back at all the struggles, all the times that person had a setback, wanted to throw the towel in, and kept going no matter what. We are not seeing all the naysayers and negative people that were encountered along the way, all the frustration, late nights, sacrifice and circumstances that were overcome. These are part of every success story.

When I achieved a top rank for the very first time, the way people looked at me changed. They were now looking up to me more than ever and wanting my guidance. The question I get asked the most is this: If I could tell them the one thing they can do to get to where I am, or exactly what I did to get to my rank, what would that be? If you are a top leader, then you already know there's no simple answer to this question. I used to think there was, but there most certainly is not. For me it's years of learning, applying, screwing up, going at it again, trial and error, building my network, overcoming obstacles, never letting anyone else's opinion sway me, resisting the urge to give up, and trusting that everything I was doing, despite the fact that it wasn't paying immediate dividends, was going to pay off big-time.

In short, it was years of struggle and consistently overcoming obstacles that led me to where I am. I know, most of you were hoping for a fast answer and simple task you can do to invoke immediate change. There is none. It's tenacity over an extended period, going hard enough, fast enough, long enough, consistently enough to make it happen. I challenge you to find a success story that doesn't include this; if you look into it deeper. Every story of massive success has struggle.

My gift to you today, is to tell you to embrace the struggle and never quit; no matter what. What you are going through now will make you stronger and develop you into a great leader; all while paving the way for others to follow in your footsteps. There is no easy road to success. Do whatever it takes; day in and day out and you'll soon be among those who have persevered and reached the top ranks.

Action Steps and Discussion:

- Make a list of everything that is giving you resistance at this time. Make a commitment to yourself that you will never allow those things to stop you. Plan ways to get past sticking points.

- Reach out to top leaders in your company and ask them to tell you their story about what they have gone through to get where they are. I think you'll find the stories to be very inspiring.

Lesson 31: Family & Friends

Most Network Marketing companies will teach that the first thing you should do is make a list of friends and family that you feel comfortable approaching, to become your first new customers or distributors. The new person then approaches family and close friends with this product, service or business opportunity, and asks them to join. I would say the vast majority of the time this strategy is a tough one because most people's friends and family do not see them as a salesperson; let alone, as someone that can help them start a successful business.

Most of our close family and friends have formed their opinions about us and would like to keep us locked inside the tiny little box they have designated for us. They do not want to see us try anything different and will go to the ends of the Earth in an attempt to "protect" us from perceived scams, pyramid schemes and overpriced products. It's so important to discuss this with new people on your team who are brand new to the industry. They need some kind of heads up before they go out there and get their dreams crushed by someone close to them and end up with Mom as their only pity customer.

To me, the best approach is avoiding your close friends and family members until you're successful enough not to care if they join. When the outcome of each situation doesn't affect you either way, that is the best time to go for it. When you have achieved enough success, your close friends and family who are open will begin to approach *you*. It's a much easier conversation when they approach you; as opposed to you pitching them out of the blue.

Where should you begin then? There's so many people out there that you can approach. Starting with acquaintances and colder market people is your best bet; in my opinion. They do not know you quite as well and will not have you in a box like your close friends and family do. You should consider prospecting the most successful people on your list first because they are usually the ones who are open minded. Begin building your business and let the ones closer to you watch and become curious. Believe me, they are watching and they will ask eventually. They will be wondering why you haven't approached them and that alone will spark their curiosity. People want what they think they can't have. The best thing you can do is not give it to them until they ask.

Action Steps and Discussion:

- What are your thoughts about approaching family and close friends about your business?

- Identify and make a list of the most successful people you know and approach them first.

- When do you feel is the best time to speak with those closest to you about how you can help them solve a problem or help them with their goals?

Lesson 32:
I'll Join You if You Join Me

This is a fun one that we have all run into. The old "I'll join you if you join me" scenario. This typically happens when you prospect somebody who is currently building another Network Marketing business; or they prospect you. Both sides end up in a "my dog is bigger than your dog" debate which ends in a standoff. Then one side comes up with the brilliant idea of joining each other which supposedly will benefit both sides. Then both affiliates join each other's business and the second standoff begins. Now that each side has joined the other, they wait and hope the other side will see the light and shift their focus. Frustration sets in when this doesn't happen and both parties cancel their auto ship for the next month.

Let's do a quick recap of what has happened here. Each person sponsored someone who didn't want to join their business. They both ordered products they didn't want. They both got frustrated with each other because neither one did anything to build the other business. They both quit the other business, and they both burned a bridge. The end result is that neither side got any benefit or value out of the entire situation. It was a complete and utter waste of time and energy.

The other side of the coin is when someone tells you that their business is the perfect complement to what you are doing and therefore you should join them. Of course, if you suggested they do the same, it's not going to happen. If it's a perfect match- shouldn't both sides join each other? Wouldn't that make sense? Maybe the products do complement each other. Even if that is the case, it takes us back to the "I'll join you if you join me" scenario that never works out.

The best resolution to this conundrum is to simply support the other person in their business either by encouraging them or becoming a customer. I always look at people in other companies as a potential customer. If they see you as somebody that supports and encourages them, and they have a need for your product or service, they are far more likely to stick around as a customer of yours. The same goes for you. If you are encouraged and supported by them, then you are much more apt to make a purchase from them as a customer.

I always preach that we should all support each other in the Network Marketing industry. This means cheering each other on and by purchasing from each other when there is a need. This shows that you really care and gives you a much better chance at acquiring a long term business partner at some point in the future. People will always join somebody with great character who was there for them.

Action Steps and Discussion:

- Reach out to people in other companies and show your support by either providing value or making a purchase as a customer.
- If you have ever been in the "I'll join you if you join me" scenario, write down and discuss all of the pros and cons of that particular situation.

Lesson 33: Sorting vs. Convincing

Keeping your pipeline full is the key to success in any business that involves sales; which is pretty much everything. It's no different in Network Marketing. You have to keep moving forward and planting seeds if you want to have a big harvest day. If you only plant a few seeds and hope that they grow, your chances of success will be slim to none.

When you only prospect a small list of people you end up in the convincing game. Instead of moving forward, you are now circling back because you placed all of your hopes on a short list of individuals. Now your only chance at acquiring a new customer or business partner is to convince somebody to take a chance. When you are in this position, it makes you look desperate. The truth is- you *will* be desperate if you are stuck on people because they are your only hope.

Real success in Network Marketing comes when you work the numbers. Your focus should never be to convince; instead, it should always be to sort. You are looking for the lookers; instead of trying to convince those that aren't looking to change their mind. This is why it's so important to always be expanding your list and making new contacts every day. With social media now at our disposal there's really no reason anyone can't add new connections and talk to new people every single day. All we want to do is make new friends and find out if they are open to looking at what we have to offer.

When you continue to move forward, simply looking for those who are open, you'll give yourself many more opportunities for success. Instead of banking on a short list of people and bugging the crap out of them, you'll learn to detach yourself from the outcome. Your focus will shift to prospecting and presenting, prospecting and presenting, prospecting and presenting... you get the idea. When you are laser focused on doing this, your follow-ups with people will not seem desperate. More people will want to join your team because they see how busy and serious you are. Your business will start to thrive.

Action Steps and Discussion:

- Make a list of people you have prospected that may possibly become your business partner or customer in the future. If the list isn't that long, you will need to work on expanding it.

- Set a goal for creating new contacts each day and hold yourself accountable for making those connections.

Lesson 34: Haters & Naysayers

They say: if you don't have any haters, then you are not doing it right. This is so true because when you start to have success in Network Marketing the haters will present themselves. They are in the wings waiting to rain on your parade because they have given up on their own dreams. Their main focus is to knock you off of your game, get you agitated, and ruffle your feathers. Whether or not you allow them to do this is your choice. Your mindset will determine how you handle the wrath of haters. You can let them bait you into pointless banter and drama, or you can use them as motivation. I suggest you choose the latter.

Naysayers are everywhere too. They seem to appear more often in the early stages of a network marketer's journey, although they really never completely disappear. Their main focus is to make you quit before you even get started. They will tell you it's a pyramid, nobody ever makes money in those things, it's a scam, and that you are wasting your time. They will give you financial advice even though they are just-over-broke. They will offer business advice even though they have never owned a business. They will act as if they know everything about Network Marketing even though they have never been involved in it and if they have, it was extremely short lived. Never allow these naysayers to slow you down or make you quit. If you do, they win.

Most haters and naysayers have either never been involved in Network Marketing or they had a bad experience and quit. It's not that they are bad people at heart; they simply do not want to see someone else succeed at something they failed at or were too afraid to try. By them attempting to knock you down, they are justifying in their own minds why they refuse to be involved. If they can only drag you down it will give them the opportunity to say "told you so" and keep you on their level.

Do not ever allow others to place limits on you and what you can accomplish. If you make the choice to never quit no matter what, commit to yourself to do whatever is necessary to get there and persevere through all of the obstacles and challenges along the way, then you can't help but to succeed. It rarely happens as fast or as easily as we want it to, yet it will happen if you make it your mission in life and back it up with consistent daily action. Keep moving past the haters and naysayers and never allow them to take your power away. You have it within you to prove them wrong and achieve massive success.

Action Steps and Discussion:

- Pay extra special attention to the way people treat you when talking about your business. If you detect a hater or naysayer take immediate action to keep your power.

- Make a concerted effort to spend more time with people who support your goals and encourage you to pursue them and spend less time with people who do not believe in you or themselves.

Lesson 35: Ranking Up

Hitting ranks is something we all strive for in Network Marketing. It gives us recognition, opens up more levels of income and signifies that we have grown as a leader and a human being. You do not reach high ranks within a company unless you have helped many other people along the way. To achieve ranks, it requires hard work, commitment, consistency, duplication and the ability to overcome challenges while maintaining your enthusiasm.

Have you heard the phrase: it's net-work marketing not net-wish marketing? This is absolute truth and when you've been in the industry long enough to take it seriously, you'll see the difference in people. Some are working while others are wishing and talking. The ones who are working hard are getting results because they have made the necessary sacrifices and are taking action daily. Those who are wishing may talk a big game about how they are going to crush it, yet in reality they are doing very little action taking. At some point, they must learn that no amount of wishing, waiting and talking is going to get them anywhere unless they start doing. The only way we learn and get better at something is by doing.

What you do on a daily basis determines your level of commitment to your business and yourself. Have you fully committed to making this happen no matter what? You will know by looking at your activities. Are your evenings spent watching TV or are you on your phone working your business? Do you go to bed early when you are tired or do you force yourself to stay up and work? Are you out partying on the weekends or are you home performing income generating activities? Your answers to these questions are the key in knowing whether or not you will be hitting the next rank soon. The top ranked leaders in your company are committed to their business above everything else. Are you?

Then, there's duplication. The ability to teach others to do what you are doing is one of the most important aspects of building a huge team. There must be a simple duplicable system that the average person can easily follow. I'm not saying they will always do it; because not everyone will, but whatever you are doing must be duplicable. A new rep should be able to come into your company and follow a system step by step, and then be able to teach more new reps to follow that same system. When people can duplicate, it creates massive momentum and you will start crushing ranks.

Action Steps and Discussion:

- Take a look at how you are onboarding new reps. Are you using the system that your company teaches and duplicating it? Or are you reinventing the wheel and doing things that are not duplicable?

- Do you have a team website or document that everyone in your team can use to illustrate step-by-step, what a new rep should do to get started? If not, get together with your top leaders and create a simple and easy to follow list of steps that anyone can do.

Lesson 36: Public Speaking

Most people have a fear of public speaking, mainly because it's outside of their comfort zone. It's not something they are used to doing or ever even aspired to do. When it comes to Network Marketing, communication and networking become important skills. The ability to confidently speak one-on-one with others is extremely important and highly beneficial to those who can do this in front of large audiences of people.

With today's technology, public speaking does not have to be done on a stage in front of a live audience. It can be done on live or recorded social media videos from the comfort of your own home. This doesn't mean it's any more comfortable to do; it's just easier for anyone who wants to do it. We no longer have to work our way up to being selected as a keynote speaker at a conference or event. We can simply whip out our smartphone and go live at any time. This is a powerful tool to build your business, yet so many people are not using it; simply because they fear what others may think.

The only way to get better at public speaking is to simply do it, and do it often. When it comes to live videos, I didn't get great at them overnight. People see me now and they think I'm a natural. The truth is that I was petrified to post my first ever recorded video; which is the way it used to be. Then, once I was used to posting recorded videos, live video was the newest thing. I had butterflies in my stomach during my first live. The reason I am great at them now is because I just kept doing them. I've done so many live videos at this point that it feels natural for me to be on camera. This is the point you need to work on getting to.

My live videos led to me being asked to speak on stage at my company's very first international convention. The audience was probably around four hundred people, which is not huge by any means, but still a full banquet room nonetheless. My experience from doing live videos on social media definitely helped me feel more comfortable on stage; although it's a totally different animal. Instead of staring at yourself on your phone or laptop screen, you are staring at an actual live audience in front of you.

Although it was an entirely different environment, I still crushed it and you can too!

Action Steps and Discussion:
- If you are not currently doing live videos on social media for your business,

plan a time to do your first one right now. Yes, you read that right you must do it.

- Tell your upline leaders and corporate office that you wish to take on speaking at an event, training or even on a call to tell your story. Start putting your face and name out there.

Lesson 37: Calls, Meetings & Events

When I first started in Network Marketing, I didn't understand the importance of getting on team calls, going to meetings and attending company events. I thought, how would getting on a weekly call, help my business in any way? Why do I need to go to a meeting and listen to people tell me to do what I thought I already knew? It's easy for them to say. Why would I spend money to attend a convention when I'm not even making money? I'll go when I'm earning enough to justify it. I am cringing as I write this, because I hear people say these things now and I know it's self-destructive. One sure fire way to fail in Network Marketing is refusing to plug in, while believing your own false justifications as to why you shouldn't. It's a recipe for never getting anywhere.

The first things you want to plug into and get your team plugged into are team calls and company calls. This is where you stay aware of what is going on within the team and company. It's important to be in the know rather than be the person who is always asking about things that have been discussed and announced. Weekly calls are also vital to raising your belief level in yourself and in what you are doing. Being surrounded by individuals who have the same vision as you is extremely encouraging. Belief is one of the most important things you can have and you do not want to detach yourself from it; ever.

Meetings and trainings are important as well; whether they are local or online. You may be telling yourself that you don't need training, as I used to do. The second you think you know everything, you will be stuck where you are. Did you ever notice that all top income earners are always in attendance at trainings and meetings? This is no coincidence. Those who are completely immersed in what they are doing are the ones who make it big. The biggest earners are the ones who are obsessed with constantly improving; no matter how far they've come. Always attend trainings and events.

Company conventions and events are huge and can be a launching pad for your business to explode. These are a sticking point for many people, as they tend to come with an investment in order to participate. There's the ticket price, hotel room, airfare, meals and other expenses. If you think this is not a worthwhile investment, you should think again. Every time I have attended an event my business has taken off. If you promote events and get all of your team members there, your business is bound to skyrocket immediately after. Everyone will leave with high belief levels and they will be super pumped up to go out and tell the world what they have to offer. This is the type of excitement you want within yourself and your entire team.

Action Steps and Discussion:

- Immediately make a commitment to yourself to be on all the calls, and attend every meeting and company event. If there's an event scheduled that you do not have a ticket for yet, put this book down and go purchase a ticket right now.

- Promote all the calls, meetings and events to your entire team. The more your team gets plugged in, the bigger and faster your business will grow.

Lesson 38:
Social Media & Smart Phones

In early days of Network Marketing, we had to do everything old school. In order to get people exposed to your products and opportunity, you would have to call them on the phone, invite them to a home party or hotel meeting, and then hope they showed up. To meet new people, we had to go out and frequent places to build our network. I'm not against good, old fashioned networking by any means; in fact, I think we should all incorporate it into our businesses. However, we now live in a time where you can meet and network with thousands of people right from the comfort of your own home.

Social media and smart phones have transformed the entire industry. Social media specifically, has opened the door to what I like to call: the largest networking group in the world. There are endless people on social media that you can start a conversation with, add them as friends and build relationships. If you simply spoke with five new people every day, just think about how many people you'll be exposing to what you do. That's one hundred fifty new people a month and eighteen hundred people a year. Increase your number to ten or twenty and you can double or quadruple how many new people you are reaching. You can sort through people very quickly; looking for the ones who are open and that you feel positive energy with. Social media also allows you to brand yourself and build a following of people by producing great contact and interacting with others. It's well worth the investment of your time to master social networking.

The introduction of the smart phone has given us all the ability to work smarter as opposed to harder. I like to call my smart phone my "office" because that's basically what it is. I can work from anywhere in the world if I have my smart phone and cellular service. It contains all of the tools I need like- websites, apps, videos, contacts, social media and more. I can give someone in another city an entire presentation standing on a beach somewhere. Texting is another great way to follow up with people and set up appointments. It seems like nobody answers their phone anymore; but most will see a text right away and respond to it. You have the ability to search for information and get answers to questions at the touch of your fingertips. I have built an empire with my smart phone and I am thankful every day for this wonderful invention. Those who master the tools we have been given with today's technology will have the ability to grow their businesses at a much faster pace.

Action Steps and Discussion:

- Make it a point to learn and master all of the social media platforms that you wish to focus on. This takes consistency and time but it will pay you huge dividends.

- Explore your smart phone and make sure you become familiar with all of the tricks and tasks it can perform to streamline your business.

Lesson 39:
Tire Kickers & Time Wasters

We've all had to deal with tire kickers and time wasters at some point in our Network Marketing careers. Training yourself to sort through people quickly can help avoid getting stuck on these types of people. They will drain your energy and time if you are not skilled enough to recognize them. This is especially true if you are not prospecting enough people; because then, they will make you fall into desperation mode, as you endlessly chase them. In our world, this is one of the saddest and loneliest places you can be.

Tire kickers will come to you, acting interested and asking questions. You will get them looking at your presentation, considering your products and even to the point where they will claim to be ready to join. Yet, they will never join. They may say soon or when the time is right, or this Friday when they get paid. Sure enough, Friday comes and they will ghost you. They may disappear for a while; days, weeks, even months, and then come back and start asking questions again. It's as if it was the first time. They will even go as far as to swear they are really ready this time. Then all of a sudden, poof, they are gone again. These people are the eternal prospects; always "interested" but never taking the leap.

Time wasters are very similar; except for the fact that they may actually join. Once they are in, all they will ever do is ask endless questions, complain about everything, blame you for their lack of progress, and then call you a scam. They will always need your time and attention to discuss various matters and will talk a big game. When it comes time to take action, you'll see they are all talk. Ironically, these are the people that require the most of your time while deserving the least.

If you want to be successful, you should spend eighty percent or more, of your time with the leaders on your team that have the most production, and the other twenty percent with everyone else. Do not allow tire kickers and time wasters to monopolize your valuable time. By the way, if you see any of these qualities in yourself, this is not meant to insult you. If this is the case, you should take it as a wake-up call to reprogram your mindset. We all have hesitation when it comes to new ways of thinking. Overcoming these mind barriers and realizing what is worth your time and what isn't, will determine your path. Focus on spending your time where it is most deserved and you will win bigger.

Action Steps and Discussion:

- Make a list of the top producers in your team and plan your schedule so that eighty percent of your time spent with people is with those who deserve it the most.

- Review your prospects and eliminate those who are only wasting your time. Cut them loose!

Lesson 40: Working From Home

When you are used to working at a nine to five job, it's easy to fantasize about how much you may enjoy firing your boss to build your Network Marketing business from home full time. After all, you bought into the dream of working part time on your fortune while you are working full time to make a living. This is one of the biggest selling points of Network Marketing; especially to prospects who are burned out on corporate America or whatever field they are in. We offer a way for them to escape the nine to five grind. The one thing they may not realize when they first get started is how much effort it will take to get there and how different it will be.

At a job, you have set hours. Typically it's forty hours a week on a set schedule such as nine to five. Most employees have to commute in their car to work and back, so the total time spent away from home may look something like leaving at 8am and arriving home by 6pm or later if there is traffic. During the work day, employees are focused on doing the specific job they were hired to do. If they do not perform well, a supervisor or boss may take disciplinary action on them. No matter how well or poorly they perform, they will still be paid the same; although they are motivated to do well enough to keep their job. Getting fired is always a possibility if there is poor performance or when a company simply decides to make changes. Most employees will do just enough to keep their jobs and not get fired. Many feel as if they deserve to be paid more, while failing to realize they are an expense in the company's eyes. They will continue to work at this job until they've either grown tired and move on to the next, or they simply resolve themselves to accepting where they are and do nothing to change it.

Working from home is an entirely different animal. It sounds great on the surface, right? When you work from home there's no alarm clock to wake up to or specific time you need to start. You can choose your own hours. There's no dress code or timed lunch hour, no supervisors or bosses. You are now your own boss and need to be self-motivated. If you don't know what to do when there's nobody there to tell you what to do, you have to figure it out yourself. If you perform poorly, you will not be fired, but your pay will also decrease because now you get paid exactly what you are worth. Your income is a direct reflection of your effort and productivity. Even without a forty hour work schedule, you'll be working way more than forty hours and you'll be working however early or late it's necessary to get things done.

Everything is on *you*. You'll need to deal with distractions like doing the laundry, letting the dogs out, straightening up, and doing other household chores. It's tough to stay focused sometimes when you work from home.

I've done both and I will tell you that by far, I enjoy being my own boss the most. Once you get a taste of time freedom, you'll work as hard as you can to make sure you never lose it. Once you have left corporate America, the thought of ever having to go back is a nightmare. Let me just say that I have no issues with people that want to work a job, it's totally fine if that is what they prefer. However, if you are like me, then you know exactly what I am talking about. I would rather work 24/7/365 for myself than nine to five for someone else. There's no other feeling like it in the world!

Action Steps and Discussion:

- Just like your job has set hours, you will need to set hours to work your business and stick to them while you are building it part-time. Prior to the start of each month, write on a calendar the hours that you'll be working and hold yourself accountable to stick to them.

- Start putting extra effort into everything that you do; including your job. This will increase your work ethic and also have a positive impact on your Network Marketing business.

Lesson 41: Build Relationships

Even though it's called Network Marketing, it's easy to make the argument that it should be called relationship marketing. Nearly everything we do is based on relationships we build with our prospects and our business partners. People join people, follow people, stay with people, and leave people. Most often, it's the strength and trust of the relationship you've built that will determine the outcome. There has to be a reason somebody would join *you* over someone else. Why should someone follow *you* and join *your* team? What do *you* have to offer them? Have you shown that you genuinely care about them? These are all important factors that many try to skip over.

Have you ever been pitched on social media or otherwise, by somebody you don't even know? Silly question, of course you have. We've all been there and know what it feels like. I am willing to bet that you didn't feel strongly about joining this person or purchasing their products; correct? This is because they have not taken the time to get to know you and it's painfully obvious that their only concern is making a sale. They have zero interest in you, what your goals are, what your needs are, and what your reason for being involved in Network Marketing is.

Some of these people will try to quickly "microwave" a relationship with you by playing a game of twenty questions and then pitching you like they suddenly know you. They will say things like: what do you do? Where do you live? Do you have a family? How many kids do you have? Great, now check out what I have for you, ok? Yeah, no thanks! As human beings, we don't feel a connection to somebody who we feel has their own best interests at heart and not ours. These people make us feel unimportant and like we are just a number to them. Who likes feeling like a number? The answer is: nobody.

When you take the time to genuinely get to know somebody and ask thoughtful questions along the way, you'll learn about what they are looking for. Over time, you will find out what their "why" is and how you can help them with your products or opportunity. When somebody feels a strong connection with you and knows that you really care, they are way more likely to join your business and stick around. Relationships are one of the major keys to building long term residual income. If you learn how to build strong, long-lasting relationships, you are well on your way to being a huge success story.

Action Steps and Discussion:

- Every time you are speaking with a prospect or team member, evaluate whether you are truly acting in their best interests. If you are not, make the necessary changes and keep working on it.

- Perform one act of kindness every day that only benefits the other person involved.

Lesson 42: Mindset is Huge

The most important thing you can ever work on is yourself. Many don't realize this when they first get started in Network Marketing. I know that I didn't. I spent most of my time watching training videos, writing my list of prospects and did a lot of busy work that got me nowhere. I was in fear of contacting people due to lack of confidence and a weak mindset, so I filled my time with tasks that would allow me to avoid talking to people. I didn't see the benefit in reading books or doing personal development. I thought I already knew what to do and that I didn't need personal development. I couldn't have been more wrong and I'm glad that I woke up and realized it.

Personal development has changed my life more than anything else. It has given me confidence, leadership, and more income than any job has ever paid me. It has made me believe that I can accomplish amazing things that I never would have dreamed of before. All of this, I gained from working on my mindset every single day. Whether it's for ten minutes or an hour; I'm always feeding positivity into my brain and learning something new. I'm constantly striving to make improvements day in and day out. Personal development is one of the most important tools a network marketer can have in their arsenal.

When you constantly feed your brain with personal development, your mindset gets stronger every single day. You will gain the knowledge and confidence that you need to build a huge Network Marketing organization. The income that this industry has brought me has been nothing short of incredible and I must say the same for my own personal development journey. It's something that I will always be thankful for having in my life. It's true when they say that mindset is ninety percent of the battle. When you win the mindset battle, it sets you up to win many more.

Action Steps and Discussion:

- What time do you currently have set aside for personal development? If you are not already doing this, set a time each day where you will be working on strengthening your mindset.

- Turn your car time into personal development time. Download an audio book app and spend every minute you are in your car, listening to personal development books.

Lesson 43: Character & Ethics

Your character says a lot about you and how far you will go in the Network Marketing industry. Sure, you can experience short term gains by doing unethical things- but it will never last. What you put out into the universe will always come back to you. Everything you do is a reflection on yourself, your company and the industry as a whole. The reason some people have a poor opinion of Network Marketing, is because they likely came across someone who was going about their business the wrong way.

Embellishing is one thing people do that they may think is helping them; but it's really not. When you first get started and are not making much income to speak of, it's perfectly fine to be honest with your prospects. You never want to make it sound as if you are rolling in the dough when you haven't even had your first profitable month yet. It's better to share the success stories of others in the business and use them for third party validation. Whatever you do, never give your prospects the impression that what you are doing is easy or a way to get rich quick. Even if they do end up joining, they will find out very quickly that you were lying and they will not be in the business very long. Always be honest with your prospects by showing them what is possible if they are willing to do the necessary work to get there.

Another unethical thing I have seen people attempt to do is steal other people's prospects. This poor tactic can be done at an opportunity meeting, in a social media group or anywhere else. This is when you approach somebody else's prospect and try to convince them that

Jerry West

it's better to join with you. Not only is this an unethical practice, it also shows that you have a scarcity mindset. There are millions of people in the world; way more than enough for all of us to build successful Network Marketing businesses. There's no reason to step in on somebody else's territory. Always maintain an abundance mindset and show people the correct and ethical way to build your business.

When you start a Network Marketing business, you are not just representing yourself; you are also representing your company and the entire industry every time you speak to somebody. It's important to keep this in mind and to maintain the highest integrity you possibly can. Others will base their opinions of what we do, on how we interact with them. Even though we teach that you shouldn't care what others think, you really should care about being ethical and professional. You should care about how you are portraying our profession to others. If you want to be respected, then you must give people a reason to respect you. Always strive to uphold the highest standards in everything you do.

Action Steps and Discussion:

- Make it a point to lead by example and show your team the correct way to go about their business. Are you portraying good character and ethics to them?

- Name some other unethical activities that should be avoided.

Lesson 44: Be an Encourager

To be hugely successful in Network Marketing, you must develop into a leader. With that, I ask you: what type of leader do you want to become? You can be a boss who pressures people and acts as if they are superior. You can act like a manager who is always checking on others activities and not doing much actual leading. You can be the silent type who isn't bossy but also isn't doing much of anything to help others. Or, you can be what I strive to be on a daily basis; an encourager.

Nobody likes the bossy type. I was once in a company where my sponsor was worse than any boss I ever had. I was being called and texted all throughout the day, being asked how many people I spoke to so far, and to report back to him what activities I had done. It was miserable and I lasted about two months in that business. What does that tell you? People join people; therefore, people also leave people. If you are hounding people and coming down on them like you are their superior, they will not be sticking around very long. They joined Network Marketing to earn additional income and possibly become their own boss; not to gain a second and even more annoying boss than the one they have at their jobs.

Managers are those who supervise the activities of others and are not practicing as they preach. When you tell your team to do something that you are not willing to do yourself, how well do you think that is going to go? I have seen people come into a business and absolutely crush it the first month. Then, in month or two, they revert to management mode because they feel as if they have done their part, and now it's time to stop and only focus on telling the team what to do. What they are not realizing, is that they have stopped leading and are now teaching their team to do the same thing. Trust me; you do not want to train your team to fall into management mode. It will surely stunt the growth of your organization.

You should always be taking action, leading by example, and upping your leadership game. People are going to do what they see you do. It's your job to encourage them by taking inspired action every single day. If you want them to be consistent, then *you* should be consistent. If you want them to always be prospecting and recruiting, then *you* should always be prospecting and recruiting. If you are stepping up and leading the way, *they* will step up and lead the way. Always act in a way that encourages your team and watch the magic happen right in front of your eyes.

Action Steps and Discussion:

- If your team did what you did today, how happy would you be?
- Do your actions encourage others to do the same, or are they repelling people?

Lesson 45:
Persistence & Perseverance

There are two things that clearly separate extremely successful network marketers from the rest of the pack. We are all given the same set of variables when we start. We have the same company, same comp plan and same products. We are offered the same training, same tools and the same system to duplicate. The only "X" factor is us and the specific circumstances we each deal with. The big question is whether anything can stop you, or if you are prepared to keep going; no matter what?

Persistence will take you further than talent ever will. There are a lot of talented people who never make it far in Network Marketing; because they are not willing to work hard enough. Network Marketing is hard work. It comes with many challenges and struggles that most people don't see coming. It's not perfect by any stretch of the imagination; Network Marketing is simply a better way. You may work long, late hours and earn little to no commissions. Many people will agree to show up at your home party, hotel meeting or online presentation, only to ghost you. You'll have customers and business partners that don't stick around. It very well may take way longer than you thought it would to achieve the level of success you had in mind when you started. If you are able to persevere through all of this and maintain the same enthusiasm, then you have an amazing chance at being successful.

You see, the natural human response to resistance is to back down and quit. It's just easier to walk away than it is to get back up, brush yourself off and keep going. I've been knocked down many, many times, and always have gotten back up to fight the next battle. It hasn't been easy, but it's been well worth every drop of blood, sweat and tears. I've started businesses that never really got started. I've built teams only to watch them crumble and wondered if I truly wanted to do this anymore. I've been through product issues, shipping issues, customer service issues, disagreeing with corporate decisions, drama between team members, cross recruiting, and have had my good name bashed in front of many. Heck, I've even had conference calls held on my behalf; where supposed leaders told their entire teams to block me on social media. You name it and I have been through it. I always persevered no matter how bad things seemed when I was going through them. When there's not a single setback that can stop you, that's when you know your goals will be reached no matter what.

Action Steps and Discussion:

- Make a list of struggles that you have gone through and still kept going. Give yourself credit for persevering and make a commitment to yourself that nothing is going to stop you.

- Think of a time when you didn't give up on a goal; even though it seemed so far away at the time, and you still managed to accomplish it. Make a commitment to persist like that all the time; no matter what stands in your way.

Lesson 46: Helping Others

As network marketers, we naturally love to help others. It's the foundation on which everything we do stands on. Without this foundation, any business, Network Marketing or otherwise, would crumble to the ground and cease to exist. In Network Marketing, we need to help others succeed in order for us to succeed. Sure, we can go out and sell a bunch of product to earn direct commissions. I know people that have a ton of direct sales to customers and make good money. This is all well and good, but if you want to work smarter and not harder, you need to help others achieve their why.

Everyone says they want to help others because that is our mantra. That is what we do as network marketers; right? It's one thing to say it and something completely different to actually *mean* it. Are you just saying you enjoy helping others or do you truly mean it? Do you actually care? People can spot a fake from a mile away. Do not be that person who pounces on an opportunity and makes somebody feel like nothing but a number. Take the time to talk to people, ask questions, and show empathy.

Have you ever spoken to somebody and gotten the feeling that they weren't really listening to you? Have you ever sensed that all somebody was thinking about is what they were going to say once you stopped talking? If all you think about is your agenda and not your prospect's needs, then you will fall flat on your face. Those who listen and genuinely care, always get much farther because they have been handed the keys to sponsoring that person. You cannot solve a problem unless you have taken the time to listen and offer a solution that shows how much you care.

If you ever want to achieve true time freedom, you must be able to leverage the efforts of many other people. Caring is the first step you must take in order to get them on board and to help them get started. Then, you must truly care about supporting and leading them along their journey. People join people and stay with people; especially those who help them and actually care.

Action Steps and Discussion:

- Analyze your recruiting tactics and determine if you are approaching people from the standpoint of how you can help them, instead of how they can help you. Make any necessary adjustments.

- Every time you are in a conversation with someone this week, make extra effort to listen to what they are saying very closely. Let them talk about themselves and resist the urge to interject. You will be surprised at what you learn and what information you can use to help them in the future.

Lesson 47: Avoid the Drama

There are several things that are inevitable when you are building a Network Marketing business and one of them is drama. In Network Marketing, we take all types of people. There's no degree that is necessary to get started in this industry; no amount of school, and no experience requirements. We accept people from all walks of life, with all types of attitudes, opinions, work ethics, and backgrounds. We place all of these people on one team and let them figure out how to work best together. With all of these different personalities meshed together in one room, there are going to be unavoidable conflicts and there is going to be drama.

The important thing to remember when this happens is that you have no control over other people's actions. You can certainly lead by example and show them the right way to do things. Ultimately it's up to them to actually follow your lead or choose to go their own way. When drama ensues, the best thing you can do is to rise above it. Block out the noise and keep working. Do not entertain or give any of your valuable time to drama and negativity. When you do this, you are showing the rest of your team that they shouldn't entertain any of it either.

When leaders in your team cause drama, the best thing you can do is to find the right time to speak with them. I highly suggest you ask questions and listen to what is going on in their world. You never know what types of battles people are fighting internally or otherwise. Do your best to listen and hear your leader out. Once they are finished speaking and pouring their heart out to you, then you can make suggestions on how they can improve their situation. Again, you can only show them how to fix a problem. It's going to be up to *them* to actually fix it.

Overall, the most important thing you can do during these drama-filled situations is level-up your leadership game. Most of your team is looking at you to see what you will do. They are watching closely to see how you will react and respond. If you continue to focus and give no attention to the dramatic situations, your team will learn to do the same. Over time, those that are committed will always be able to block out the noise and focus on building the business.

Action Steps and Discussion:
- Review your current team activities and determine if there's any

drama that currently needs to be avoided. Make sure you and your leaders are aware of any noise that needs to be ignored.

- If there's any drama being initiated by leaders in your team, set up time for a call and let them air it out. Make suggestions for possible solutions.

Lesson 48: Abundance vs. Scarcity

The mentality that you have towards the number of opportunities that you have to gain new team members is extremely important. You can either view them as limited or endless. Have you ever heard somebody say that they've already spoken to everyone they know? Or that nobody they know is interested? These are prime examples of a scarcity mentality. In order to truly be successful, you must learn to adopt a mentality of abundance. When you have an abundance mentality, there are no shortages.

Owning a scarcity mentality is one of the sure fire ways to limit the amount of success you can have. There are a number of ways that one can operate in a scarcity mentality. Have you ever thought to yourself: if this person leaves, my business will crumble? If you ever feel that your business is dependent on any one person, you are operating out of scarcity. You should always be focused on building new legs and growing new teams so that you are not dependent on just one. Have you ever gotten angry or upset because somebody you were prospecting decided to join with someone else? If you allow things like this to consume you, then you are operating out of scarcity.

You should always be focused on abundance. When you focus on abundance, you will attract more into your life and business. When someone leaves your team, and this will happen, you should always wish them the best. There's no reason to burn that bridge when you are operating with abundance. When a prospect joins someone else in your company or another, you should congratulate them. It's a personal decision; who people decide to join with and no single person can make or break your business. You are going to do this with or without them because you know there's no shortage of people in this world. Abundance allows you to keep moving forward and focus on the next person because there will *always* be a next person. Never dwell on the ones who got away; always look for the next one.

Action Steps and Discussion:

- Review your current team and determine if you are focusing on abundance or scarcity. You'll know if you look at your downline and it's mostly dependent on one single person.

- Practice thinking in abundance and seeking it out every single day. The more you think about abundance, the more it will be attracted to you.

Lesson 49: Become a Problem Solver

Have you ever heard the phrase "stop selling and start helping"? I'm willing to guess that you have, because most of us are doing one or the other. We are either focused on our agenda and what we have to offer, or we are listening to our prospects in order to see how we can solve a problem. The issue with being mainly concerned with *our* agenda is that we don't know what we are trying to solve. We can talk about how great our products and opportunity is all day long. If we do not know how it applies to helping our prospects solve a problem, then we are wasting our breath.

When all you care about is making a sale, your prospects can see right through that. When you are mostly talking and not listening, or only care about what it is you need to say next, you are only attempting to sell something. It would be great if we could walk into a meeting, presentation or one-on-one with a prospect and just go about our business. You could simply do the same presentation every single time without even knowing why your audience should care. After all, you have the best life-changing products and compensation plan in the world; right? This would work great if everyone was the same as you. I have a news flash for you, they are not.

Everyone is different and has their own set of problems; their own journey, and their own reasons for looking at your company. The most important thing is to find out what those reasons and problems are, so that you can solve them. When you sit down one-on-one with a prospect, your focus should be on them. Let them speak and make it all about them. Ask questions and allow them to do most of the talking about themselves and why they believe you may be able to help. While you are doing this, you are learning all about how you can help them solve their problems. They are basically handing you the keys that you need to get them started.

Action Steps and Discussion:

- Look at the current way you are approaching people and determine if you are more focused on pitching your agenda, or if you are learning how you can solve their problems.

- Adjust your one-on-one presentations to focus mostly on listening to what your prospects needs are. Focus on how you and your company can help them to accomplish these things.

Lesson 50:
Make Yourself Available and Dependable

While it's true that nobody is going to build your business for you except for you, it's still great to have upline leaders who are available and dependable. These are two qualities that you should strive to have as you grow into a leadership role yourself. Nobody wants an upline that sponsors them and then leaves them in the dust. People feel burned when endless promises are made in order to convince them to join and then, once they do, the sponsor disappears. Even worse, their sponsor commits to doing a call, meeting or training, and then doesn't show up. Do not be this person.

I pride myself on always being available and approachable to everyone in my team. Yes, I do spend the vast majority of my time with those who are running with me. I still have time leftover for anyone who needs it. I'm usually just a text or phone call away. I love hearing my team talk about how responsive I am and how much it is helping them. They may not always like the answers I give; but nobody can say that I don't tell it like it is. The truth is always the best advice; whether somebody wants to hear it or not. Always tell people what they need to hear, not what they want to hear. It may hurt sometimes, but they will get over it soon enough and receive the intended message. They will appreciate the fact that you were accessible and willing to help them.

I cannot stress enough, the importance of being dependable. When you say you are going to do something, make sure you do it. When you agree to attend a meeting or to be on a call, make sure you are there. Nothing is more frustrating than dealing with someone who talks about doing things and doesn't actually do them. A leader's dependability speaks volumes about them. The very best of the best make commitments and always keep them. You do want to be known as someone who can be counted on, correct? Always stick to your obligations whether you feel like it or not. Your team will have a ton of appreciation for you and your reputation will be outstanding!

Action Steps and Discussion:

- If you have ever skipped out on a meeting, call or task that you committed to doing, reach out to the person you disappointed and own up to it. Apologize and commit to not doing it again.

- If you find yourself ignoring texts and messages make a concerted effort to respond to every inquiry by the end of each day. You owe this to your team.

Lesson 51: Shiny Ball Syndrome

We've all seen it happen and perhaps have even caught on to this ourselves. Someone joins your team and starts building. For a few months they are blowing it up and creating massive momentum. Then their initial enthusiasm for the business starts to waiver; things slow down, or something happens that throws them off of their game. Meanwhile, something new has emerged and is gaining visibility on social media. People are proclaiming this is the next best thing, big leaders are joining and building this on the down low, the timing is perfect, and you don't want to miss this. The next thing you know, your new business partner, or maybe even you, jump to the new opportunity. This is called Shiny Ball Syndrome and it's a disease that can spread like wildfire. You want to avoid it at all costs.

Many people of varying degrees of success miss out on making it big-time because they are always allowing the next shiny ball to distract them. They uproot themselves and start again, uproot themselves and start again, uproot themselves and start again... you get the idea. They are always stopping their growth at the first sign of adversity to start something else that looks better and easier. Even though they have done this time and time again, they continue to do it in a vicious cycle. I see people that are still doing this from years ago when I first decided to bring my Network Marketing onto social media. Then I see others, like me, who learned that lesson and are now massively successful because they decided to focus. They made the choice to overcome struggles and figure things out, instead of always avoiding them by leaving for a new deal.

I have been through it all. In my first Network Marketing company, I underestimated the amount of effort I would need to put in. I sponsored a few people and thought they would build it for me; but they never did. Then I joined another company at the same time, a shiny ball, thinking that two side streams of income would be better than one. However, neither was producing income and all I ended up with was multiple auto-ships. Then I started jumping from company to company every few months. I was shiny ball hopping; making a little money here and there, but never sticking around long enough to build something meaningful or to have anyone take me seriously.

It wasn't until I made the decision to commit to one business and block out all the rest of the noise, that I truly found success. I was finally able to grow into a better networker and leader by overcoming setbacks instead of repeatedly jumping away from them. I had to ignore many pitches and shiny balls to accomplish this. The more I focused on growing *one* Network Marketing business, the better of a leader I became and the more seriously I was taken by my colleagues.

Action Steps and Discussion:

- If you are currently involved with a company that serves you well and you feel passionate about, make a long term commitment to build that one company and grow within it.

- If what you are currently doing isn't serving you or you are involved in multiple deals at the same time, take the time to find one business you can fully commit to for the long term.

Lesson 52: Never Quit

The one surefire way to fail in Network Marketing is to quit. When you first join the industry, there's a whole new set of skills that need to be learned and mastered. Products and presentations are designed to get us into a company. The one thing that can make you stay and grow as a person and as a leader is you. Many people quit at the first sign of adversity or struggle because it's easier. It's easy to bow out and think to yourself that these things don't work. Your struggle will be over, you'll have no more discomfort, and there will be no shortage of supporters to reaffirm your choice.

The question is: will you allow yourself to quit? If you are the type of person who quits easily, your chances of being successful in Network Marketing are slim to none. You have to be someone who decides that they are going to do this; no matter what stands in their way. Believe me, there are many obstacles out there that are trying to stop us on a daily basis. It can be other quitters trying to drag you out with them, naysayers telling you that you are in a pyramid scheme, trusted oved ones trying to convince you to get a "real job", and even broke people who are offering you income advice. There's no shortage of experts and supporters on the quitting highway.

If you decide to stick around and go the extra mile, many times you'll find the highway to be clear of traffic. This is the road less travelled because it's the more difficult one. Most of the other drivers are telling you not to go there; to pull over your vehicle and that it's not worth the risk. You *must* keep driving. There are potholes, speed bumps, lane closures, construction and unexpected twists and turns. Still, you *must* keep driving. Those who never quit, always make it far. Decide today, that you will go the extra mile, overcome all of the obstacles on the road less travelled and never, ever quit.

Action Steps and Discussion:

- Make a list of all of the times you wanted to quit and kept going. Give yourself credit for overcoming those times and commit to always keep going; no matter what.

- You have what it takes to make it to the top *if* you will decide right now, that nothing and nobody can stop you. Decide right now and make the commitment!

Testimonials:

I promised some of my Network Marketing friends who wrote testimonials for me, that I would include them in this book, along with their name. Here they are below. Enjoy!

"I love how quickly you always respond to any question!"

– Kathy Heberle

"I love how you always respond to everyone that comments on your posts and Facebook live [videos]. You are truly an amazing leader to all."

– Julie Fowler

"Jerry is a phenomenal mentor and teacher and is continuously providing inspiration, motivation and knowledge; adding value to me on a daily basis. His encouragement has helped lead me in the right direction to persuade me in following my dreams."

— Krissy George

"Jerry is not my upline, however he has continually inspired and motivated me to follow his lead. He's given me valuable personal mentorship which I will forever be grateful for. Keep growing leaders Jerry!"

— Sarah Rhodes

"You have motivated me to see that no matter what obstacles are put in my path, there's always a way around it. Thank you for being available to help others succeed."

— Tracey Mousseau

"Your positivity inspires and keeps me going. Thank you."

    – Robbi Weeks

"Jerry West, unbeknownst to him, directly has been a true inspiration to myself and my Team. We all follow Jerry daily for his leadership and social media expertise, plus inspirational and motivational posts. His background and story are close enough to mine that I personally am inspired at knowing, I can achieve the same success he has carved out for himself and countless others."

    – Dave Miller III

"I like how engaged you are with us and with your live audience. You have a true love and compassion for helping and encouraging others. Thank you for your mentorship."

    – Laura Lee Mahoney

"I have known Jerry since his beginning in Network Marketing. Watched him grow and learn through this journey. He has been a true inspiration sharing his journey. I love how he took to Facebook for attraction marketing. He became UNSTOPPABLE and never quit!!!"

– Linda Catalano

"I was naturally drawn to your positivity. I began watching your videos, your posts, seeing how you do things and listening to your advice on how to [and] what not to do. I draw value from you every day! Thank you!"

– Michelle Daily

"I've known Jerry for years, honesty he's always been one of my top 5 mentors in the MLM arena. He's full of knowledge, never scared to try outside of the box marketing techniques and keeps things fun and interesting."

– Sarah Carbary

"Jerry was one of the first leaders I met in Network Marketing when I started my journey as a total newbie to the industry! He has set a great example to follow and has been an integral part of inspiring me to stick with it!"

– Amy Groff

"You are such a great leader! You and your videos have kept me going strong and stay positive each day. Love your wisdom and advice on how to grow our business. I have learned so much from you in such a short time [since] we have been friends. Looking forward to many more. Many Blessings to you my friend!"

    – Lou Woodward

"I am still new to this Network Marketing, but so far you've been very helpful and give great advice! I feel like every time you do a video I learn more and more. Great job!"

    – Kacy Miller-Jennings

"I've been an entrepreneur for 25 years and one of the most important attributes you can bring to the table for sales is sincerity. Jerry embodies this, to believe in yourself and the product. The world is your oyster to open."

– Kitty Garrity

"You're a true inspiration not only to me, but everyone you come in contact with that is willing to listen. The wealth of information that you share helps so many people who truly want to be a better person or want to have a successful business. Learning from someone like you is truly a treasure that can last a lifetime!"

– Kristine Schultz-Morgan

"You have shown me Jerry, that no matter what obstacle lays in your path...there is always a way around it. You are a true inspiration for all that can be achieved. Thank you."

    – Leesa Maree

"I get great value out of all your posts and videos. You are always positive and offer tips and suggestions to help anyone build their networking business!"

    – Carmel McRury

"Jerry is a great Ambassador to the Network Marketing Profession....constantly cheering on others regardless of their company. It has been fun watching him work his way to the top. Truly well-deserved brother. Keep up the great work."

    – Wesley Anderson

"You're a straight shooter, my friend, there is no sugar coating what so ever and I thank you for that. One thing I can take away from all of your videos is this: We all fail at some point in life but what we take away from that life lesson is this: You can get up and you can work harder by taking that step to keep moving forward. Life isn't easy it was never meant to be; it's called life. Network Marketing is work and it's hard work and if you put the time in and give it your 150% daily you will achieve your goals. Getting to the top is hard but staying at the top is even harder. But the reward at the end of the day is so exciting knowing you helped so many wonderful people achieve the goal of financial freedom [and] you also came from the rat race."

– Christopher Satterlee

"Jerry once published a post on Facebook that stated: 'I like all of your posts even if you don't like mine.' This statement really resonated with me. It's such a simple way to support people and to build relationships. Ever since that day, I click the like button on every single one of Jerry's posts that I see and I like so many more posts in general now just because it's such an easy way to connect with others and to show your support for your social network. Thanks Jerry!"

— Michelle Dieber

"Jerry you have been there for me - at all hours of the day (and night) - and not once did you make me feel like I was bothering you. And for those of you who don't know this, Jerry is not my upline - but he treated me as if I was a personal recruit of his!"

— Sandie Thibodeaux

"I love your great mindset and you have made me a believer that anything is possible if you believe in yourself. Your belief that limited beliefs and playing small are not conducive to a well lived life. You've opened my eyes to greater things and more is possible if you stop believing all the garbage that is holding you back from reaching your potential."

– Kathy Davidson

"Jerry West is not only an inspiration on how positive thinking can benefit your life and career but he is also a fantastic leader! He is always willing to help those around him even when it's not benefiting him. He inspires me daily with all the value he adds to social media and reminds me to work hard and to always put my best face forward!"

– Jessica Malloy

"Jerry's point of view towards Network Marketing is like a breath of fresh air. His knowledge and expertise has inspired me to push even harder to achieve my goals. Thank you for your friendship and positivity!"

– Carol Kenyon

"Great Man! Great information always! Down to earth. Has inspired me to be the best me I can be and spread that to others by inspiring them to be the best they can be. Thanks Jerry for being you."

– Gina Woodhouse

"Learning more how to be more positive by listening to you. You are an inspiration to me and others as well. No nonsense guy."

– Carmen White

"Jerry is one of the most helpful people I have met in Network Marketing. I know that when I watch his videos I will be filled with positivity and VALUE!"

– Polly Tobin

"From someone down under I can honestly say tapping into Jerry has added true value by sparking positive reflection within me and shedding light on aspects I hadn't realized before. Even with all my years of experience, life skills and nose in books - having been in MLM's for a number of years too. There is always a new or different perspective!"

– Gail Jones

"I've known Jerry through this business a few short months. I value the videos and trainings you provide to all of us, keeping it real and open for all to use. You are inspiring to many and I have had fantastic comments regarding how great you are off many in my team, heads up to you Jerry for supporting and helping us grow. A true leader in this business."

– Belinda Dawson

"Jerry is very personable and uses humor well. He inspired me by just being himself, genuine, kind and caring."

– Jacqollyne Keath

"Jerry has been absolutely amazing on how much valuable content he provides [to] us for free. Great work and please don't stop."

– Ida Ahmet

"I have been in a lot of different companies over the years. It was not until I connected with Jerry that I felt at home. This is the first time ever an upline has actually took a serious interest in my success. I'm feeling very grateful that we connected. I have become a better marketer and better person thanks to Jerry."

– Will Blohm

For Network Marketing tips and advice, I invite you to follow and connect with me on FB:

Facebook.com/JerryWest.biz
Facebook.com/52LessonsBook

You are invited to join the official...
"52 Lessons from Network Marketing"
Facebook group.

Enter to WIN a FREE personal coaching call with Jerry West! To enter:
Post a selfie holding a copy of this book and use **#52LessonsBook**

To purchase more copies of this book for you and your whole team please visit:
www.52LessonsBook.com

94843426R00121

Made in the USA
Middletown, DE
22 October 2018